Radiant Whisperings

live into your light

A Faith-Based Journaling Experience
For a Fruitful Life

Carol J. Adkins

He-*ART* Prints

Ever notice that everything we touch leaves a print? This especially shows up on a dirty car, sticky fingers leaving smudges on the fridge, walls, furniture, etc.
With each touch,
we leave our imprint which is our identity.
Some people find these quite annoying as they keep busy cleaning the finger prints off to reveal cleanliness. Others, perhaps, new Mothers and Grandmothers, love seeing these prints everywhere as a reminder of a little one's love.
He-*ART* prints are a reflection of the person who leaves them behind. As we go forth on life's journey,
let your Heart leave
a memorable touch on someone by showing your act of compassion, love and kindness on those you come in contact with each and every day.
Through these small acts of imprinting He-*ART* touches, may they receive your love and they too can pass it on.
Sometimes someone touches our hearts and can stay there forever.

Radiant Whisperings

live into your light

Biblical resources KJV, NKJV
Cover art by: Sabina & Andreas Thaler

Radiant Whisperings

live into your light

those who look to him are radiant; their faces are
never covered with shame.

Psalm 34:5

This Radiant Whisperings
Journal Belongs To:

What I tell you in darkness, speak in the
light, and what you hear whispered in the ear,
proclaim on the housetops.
Matthew 10:27

faith Thoughts

The original Thoughts to Ponder, was inspired and written by author Neva Hardy. This compendium of verses is still being published monthly for her Church's newsletter, the "Son" shine flyer. This seed had been planted in 1987 and spanned 'til 2012. Part of this collection was printed 20 years ago for family and friends to enjoy.

This full collection is being compiled into two books by her daughter, Carol J. Hardy Adkins, to broaden the reach of viewers, and provide inspiration and pleasure for anyone who reads them. Carol and her 2 brothers and 2 sisters, grew up on a century farm near Winthrop, Iowa, witnessing their Mother's creative writings, amongst her Hardy cooking and other talents. The Hardy lineage goes back to 1885 from Lincolnshire, England, when our forefather, Pridgeon Hardy, came and purchased a farm. He helped build the First Congregational Church in Winthrop, Iowa, by hauling rocks for the foundation using a team of horses and wagon. Six generations have attended and sat in our favorite pew. How times have changed from farming with horses to using big equipment.

Eventually, this Church merged with the local Methodist Church and became the Church of Christ United. In recent years, another new addition had to be built in this small rural community of just over 800. Being an artist, I have found a new way of preserving pieces of our heritage by sharing these seed reflections to grow a new fruitful season as a gift from the Hardy He-*art*. A sideline passion is collecting meaningful and inspirational sayings which I will blend in with the Thoughts. We are reminded how things have changed and how constant the life line has remained.

Through this art of preserving, may the words of life remind us of the rich fullness and abundance of our lives. See what memories stir up for you and how these timeless verses translate to today's world.

The Grandma Window

9/13/2014 by Carol J. Adkins

The engine is running and patiently awaits its turn around the vast, gravel driveway. The last goodbyes, hugs, and money have been exchanged. Now slowly, the car begins to navigate around the ever present light pole of the Hardy farm. The light from above casts a beam my way. A quiet savoring of tranquility and sweet serenity of past memories, open spaces, sunrises and sunsets, quickly soak up my thoughts.

I see the reflection in the rear view mirror of a family tree that has grown such Hardy roots so deep in this rich soil. It seems an impossible task to let something so fruitful be harvested into a brand new crop. The tires of the heavy laden car do not want to leave this space. They enjoy listening for the echo sounds of their cousins-the wheels of the John Deeres. But, they too, have faded into glory as well.

As dusk settles in, the headlights provide a warm glow and illuminate the familiar landscape. This light beckons attention on everything it sees. Images of work, play, guests, strangers, neighbors, relatives, the alpha and the omega, the ties that bind, the Hardy century farm, a ritual, a destination, a loving Hardy meal. The car has turned its final curve and now has come to a rolling pause. A gentle breeze has come floating in my open window-bringing forth the memories of a gift to treasure.

A final glance at the house, a cornerstone, a haven, a Christian home. Now, wait for it! And there it is! An extra goodbye send off with a smile as big as the farm. A love that will never leave-the special place in your heart so well cared for. This window will be closing for this season in time. A new window will soon open-sending in the gentle breeze of memories with it.

This once occupied Grandma window from generations past to present-has a touchstone for our souls. The heritage is strong, faithful, and the blessings are abundant. New windows, new soil, will continue to reap what has been sowed. Grandma's' house may be where the best legacy resides, but where the cookie jar and love are always plentiful. The engine is now ready to roll and find its new path to explore. The love from the Grandma window resides in us all.

After living on the farm for 67 years, Author Neva Hardy, age 90, sold the century Hardy farm and built a condo in town. Legacy photo by Granddaughter Blaire Gladwin

Hardy He-*Arts*

You are the light that can create your circle of love and faith to flow through and bind your life legacy together. Let this collection of motivational, light hearted, easy to read and rooted in Biblical truths, help spark your journey to add a spiritual growth ring to your legacy. Each Thought contains faith, hope and love concepts. May you find the beauty in all of God's creations in every season on your faith path. Make this moment a living footprint of love and be the ***Keeper of Light*** for the next generations.

Celebration of the Hardy Legacy

Reverend Clarissa Martinelli

Ms. Carol Adkins, The Keeper of the Neva Hardy Legacy, has put a compilation of wise sayings, inspirational quotes, poems and proverbs from her enlightened, intelligent, and forward-thinking Mom, Ms. Neva, regarding important aspects of life. Compiled and arranged to give the reader encouragement and hope in life based on their underlying and internal needs, wants and desires. Everyone on Earth is special; everyone is unique. Nobody past, present, or future has gone through or has had the same thoughts and experiences as you, nor will they in the future. As a result, you see the world in a completely unique way.

We pray this inspirational book will guide your mind's eye in distinguishing the most impacting and transformative passages to you and your being as well as reaffirming or contradicting what you already know and/or believe. Out of the numerous inspirational quotes, poems and proverbs within this book, your personality will subconsciously pick out the most relevant ones to you and you alone. It would be a mistake to concentrate on only one subject because all the readings are connected to aid you in reaching your own epiphany (an intuitive grasp of reality through something (such as an event) usually simple and striking.)

Ms. Carol's hope for this collection of Mom's wisdom is enlightenment; to assist the readers in realizing what is truly important in life, as well as to find their version of true self; to find their true inner being; to find purpose; and, most importantly discover what makes them and them alone happy.
We hope you will fully immerse yourself in self-discovery-not only through reading, but through journaling, coloring, drawing, and conversation.

Ms. Neva believed that words have a powerful ability to guide us through life's journey, and with just a little inspiration, we can change our focus, gain clarity, and move in a new direction. Be inspired to live a brighter, happier, and more positive life.

On Mother's Day, 2023, the first book, Keepers of Abundance, how deep are your roots, was gifted to the Women of 5th Avenue United Methodist Church, West Bend, Wi. by Reverend Clarissa Martinelli.

Leaving a Legacy

What are the most important lessons you've learned in life?

_____
_____
_____
_____
_____
_____

What advice would you pass on to those who come after you?

_____
_____
_____
_____
_____
_____
_____

How do you want to be remembered?

_____
_____
_____
_____
_____
_____

 Be the light Matthew 5:14

My Living Legacy

What ways can you preserve your legacy one day at a time.

_____
_____
_____
_____
_____

What ways do you feed your soul by expressing positive emotions, like love, joy, gratitude and passion?

_____
_____
_____
_____

How will you make a difference in your lifetime?

_____
_____
_____
_____

My Story

_____

_____

_____

_____

_____

_____

_____

_____

_____

_____

_____

_____

_____

_____

_____

_____

_____

_____

My Story

Contents:

Smorgasbord of Sorts

The holidays this past month have
been like a smorgasbord of sorts.
Most people attend parties, social affairs and family
gatherings. The food served is appetizing, comforting,
filling and very tempting.
You want to try a sample of this or that and go back for a
larger helping of your favorites.
God sets a smorgasbord before us every day.
If we need comfort, healing, strength, advice, courage, love,
forgiveness, patience or just a friend He is always available.
Sometimes we only need Him for a short time.
Other times a crisis, a death or a serious health problem
and we need Him night and day.
He is there for whatever prayer you need answered.
He wants us to be filled with his goodness and mercy
and we need to
praise him back for all these blessings.

You shall eat your fill and bless the Lord your God.
Deuteronomy 8:7-8

Ponder: God wants spiritual fruit, not religious nuts.

Today I am grateful for

Ponder Time

Be the light

Time for Jubilation

On New Year's Eve a man at a church
service in Waterloo, Iowa said they were
celebrating the new millennium and also a
Jubilee Year.
A Jubilee year occurs every 50 years.
The Catholics even have a new Jubilee logo they are
promoting. It is a blue circle representing the universe and a
need for solidarity. Separating colored straight lines stand for
the cross with a light in the center for Christ who is the light of
the world. Five colored doves that represent the continents
encircle the light. The colors of the logo remind us that joy and
peace are an integral part of the Jubilee celebration.
Jubilee years are meant to be times dedicated in a special
way to God. We do this best by living our Christian vocation
to the fullest in the spirit of the law and the beatitudes.
It is a time for unity, peace, forgiveness and social justice.
But it is also a time for jubilation and joy.
The joy is from receiving the
Good News that came to us in and through Jesus Christ.
We are commissioned to be followers of Christ and make the
Good News known to all nations. Let's respond in whatever
way we can to bring joy and peace.
But God's mercy is so abundant, and his love for us
is so great. Ephesians 2:4
Satisfy us in the morning with your unfailing love, that we may
sing for joy and be glad all our days. Psalm 90:14

Ponder: Peace starts with a smile.

Today I am grateful for

Become the Change

Ponder Time

Be the light

Gift of Salvation

Six miners were working 1500' below the
surface when a shaft suddenly collapsed.
Debris trapped one of their companions.
Then mud and water began to rush in.
If the other men had tried to rescue him they would have
put their own lives in jeopardy. They were forced to abandon
him and free themselves.
This was a heart wrenching decision they had to make.
Christ knows the feeling of being abandoned.
While he was hanging on the cross he pleaded to God,
"My God, my God,
why hast thou forsaken me?" Mark 15:34
God must have felt like these miners to have to turn his
back on his precious Son. He could have spared him but
we wouldn't have
the gift of salvation.
Fortunately, God never turns his back on anyone. We can
experience again and again the reality of his promise,
"I will not fail you or forsake you."

Ponder: "If Christ is not Lord of all,
                        then He is not Lord at all."

Today I am grateful for

Let's make today beautiful

Ponder Time

Be the light

Promise of Hope

The Easter lily starts out with a bulb in the earth
and at the appropriate time bursts forth with new life.
It is symbolic of the life of Jesus after he was crucified,
buried and rose from the dead to
his new resurrected life.
The leaves are green for new life and the blossom is white
for purity. The shape of the lily is a trumpet, which heralds
spring's arrival and new hope. The sepal is yellow signifying
Christ is the light.
No wonder it is the favorite flower for Easter,
one of the most holy days for Christians.
It is the symbol and promise
of hope
that mankind's soul is immortal.

Ponder: From the smallest hope and wishes,
the greatest dreams take root.

Today I am grateful for

Believe in Yourself

Ponder This

Be the light

Good Times and Bad Times

After Jesus' resurrection, the
disciples were enthralled with following Christ.
They devoted their time to starting churches and
changing people's' lives.
When we become a Christian we have more enthusiasm
and spark and later we tend to lose some of the initiative.
When a calamity or tragedy strikes a community people turn
out to help in many ways. Believers in God attend church
more often and pray in these circumstances. They sense a
deep need for a divine intervention, comfort or healing.
They also give more in benevolences.
However, we should pray for people in both good and bad
times. God loves and cares for us just the same when we
are at our worst or when we are doing something good.
We shouldn't forget to give him thanks for answered prayer
after a crisis and day to day blessings.

Behold, I am the Lord, the God of mankind;
is there anything too hard for me?
Jeremiah 32:27

Today I am grateful for

BE
KIND

Ponder Time

Be the light

Your Reward Ticket

It seems we have a
tendency to expect rewards
for just about everything–the children get
good grades, excel in sports or any field and
adults are no different.
Does God reward us for every good endeavor?
He smiles his approval and we are no doubt blessed.
Does he punish us for every sin we commit?
We get corrected and are given another chance.
Maybe we should follow God's example and give a smile
of approval instead of promising rewards.
It gets to the point where we expect bigger rewards and
may go into debt to try and keep up with friends.
Christ died on the cross for our sins.
The greatest reward we can ever have is
to accept him as our Savior.
This reward is our ticket into heaven.
Earthly things will never get us past the pearly gates.
Make the Lord your first priority
and everything else will find its proper place.

Every good thing bestowed and every perfect gift is
from above coming down from the Father. James 1:17

For God so loved the world that he gave his only
begotten Son, that whosoever believeth
in him should not perish
but have everlasting life. John 3:16

Ponder Time

___ / ___ / ___

Decision Time

Rejoice

Renew your soul

No Waiting Period

Most everyone carries insurance for all kinds
of things including property, health, life, car, etc.
We can even get fined if we don't carry our car
insurance coverage in the car at all times.
Most policies have a deductible and even then they don't
cover 100%. But if we don't have insurance, the bills can
really be outrageous and the first thing someone wants
to sue even if they think they are not guilty of wrongdoing.
There usually is a waiting period to be accepted.
Sometimes we can be rejected for pre-existing conditions.
But God gives us assurance that he will care for us
and deliver us and no waiting period.
After our words of confession and reflection during Sunday
morning worship, we have the words of assurance to know
we are
forgiven.
Throughout the Bible the people were backsliders but God
still cared for them and expected them to return his love.
We are to learn from their mistakes and our own that
God's assurance is 100%.

Ponder: A Sunday School teacher was testing her class on
the Ten Commandments. She asked, "Can anyone recite a
commandment with only four words in it?"
A little boy raised his hand immediately. "I know," he said.
"Keep off the grass."   —Brenton

Today I am grateful for

TRUST THE TIMING OF YOUR LIFE

Ponder Time

Be the light

We All Have Choices

"The eyes of the Lord are in every place,
keeping watch on both the evil and the good."
-Proverbs 15:3

We may think what we say or do in private is no concern to others. But God is watching all the time. There is no place we can hide from him. "His eyes search back and forth across the earth looking for people whose hearts are perfect towards him so that he can show his great power in helping them." 2 Chronicles 16:9

Starting in childhood we are inclined to put the blame on someone else for our errors. Adult crimes have excuses that go back to their upbringing and try to give an account and try to get out of the sin they find themselves in.

We all have choices whether they are good or evil.
Someday we are going to give an account to the Lord for our thoughts and actions.

We will be found guilty because He is the only true judge.
He is a God of mercy and forgiveness
if we repent of our sins.
He expects us to go and sin no more.
We should learn from our mistakes and not blame anyone but ourselves.

Ponder: When we get tangled up in our problems, be still.
God wants us to be still so He can untangle the knot.

Today I am grateful for

All THINGS are POSSIBLE

Ponder Time

_____

_____

_____

_____

_____

_____

_____

_____

_____

Be the light

Fame or Money

The Summer Olympics have been in full swing in Sydney, Australia. Over 10,000 athletes from 199 countries are competing. Many of the athletes were disqualified because of cheating on drugs. Newer methods of drug testing have made it easier now to detect that which used to go unnoticed. Some countries started 8 or 9 year olds with injections or pills to better their chances of winning. What a disappointment to the athletes to work so hard and be shamed into leaving because they were forced to take them. Now that some athletes are past competing the side effects have ruined their health.

Some very young children that were picked as potential athletes have been trained away from home and have missed their childhood and growing up with their families.

Our body is a temple of God and we should not destroy it for fame or money. What a waste of a good healthy body to be ruined for early death or a life of misery.

Cheating doesn't pay in any walk of life. Sooner or later it will be found out and your name ruined. It may involve not only your own life but your family's as well.

As every person hath received the gift, even so minister the same one to another, as good stewards of the manifold grace of God. 1 Peter 4:10

Ponder: Living on Earth is expensive, but it does include a free trip around the sun.

Today I am grateful for

Choose Peace

Ponder Time

Be the light

Refill My Cup

Every time we turn around we need a refill
of something. Maybe it's the gas tank, prescription
drugs, groceries, etc. Usually the price goes up faster than
our budget allows. This winter with heating costs rising many
will feel the added crunch.
God tells us any time we need a refill of love, strength and
comfort, our cup can overflow at no extra cost. Jesus paid the
price for us so we need to put our trust in him to supply our
needs. He reminds us that he feeds the birds of the air and
clothes the flowers in splendor.

John 10:10 promises— "I have come that they may have life
and they may have it more abundantly."
Every day is a new gift.
There are many priceless gifts that money can't buy.
Praise God for your blessings and be thankful.

Give thanks to the Lord, for He is good; For His loving
kindness is everlasting. Psalms 136:1

God's love has been poured out into our hearts. Romans 5:5

Today I am grateful for

you are
AMAZING

Ponder Time

Be the light

Our Future Plans

Mary and Joseph had probably made plans for their future. However, God intervened and they were to carry out the Master's plan.

Mary, no doubt, worried if the baby would arrive during their several days' journey plodding along on a donkey. When they did arrive in Bethlehem there was no room in the inn. God preferred they have privacy away from the noise and bustle of the inn. He chose a stable for them with warmth from the animals. A humble birth for a King and then have it first announced to lowly shepherds.

How strange!

Even the hasty flight into Egypt was part of God's plan. He provided for their security and provisions until it was safe to return home.

God has great plans for each of us. Sometimes we rush ahead of him and do not wait for his direction. Usually something fails or we get distracted. Being patient is not one of our virtues.

Slow down and pray about his plans for your future. They may exceed any of your expectations.

"Mercy unto you, and peace, and love, be multiplied."
Jude 1:2

Ponder: Blessed are the flexible for they shall not be bent out of shape.

Today I am grateful for

THE LORD IS MY
Light
AND
Salvation

PSALM 27:1

Ponder Time

Be the light

Warehouse of Blessings

This time of year many stores are having
end of the year sales or taking inventories. Quite
often they may be closed for a day or two to get ready.
Old merchandise needs to be reduced in order to fill
the shelves with new items. Many stores even have
specials year round.
How does God keep track of all his inventory? He must
have a huge warehouse of blessings that don't even get
asked for. How can he even give them to people if they
don't pray about it?
His word says he's open for business 24 hours a day.
We humans can't even compete with that.
His warehouse can also contain good and bad things.
Job 38:22, "Have you entered the treasury of snow, or
have you seen the treasury of hail, which I have reserved
for the time of trouble, for the day of battle and war?"
The rest of the chapter deals with wind, rain, lightning,
frost, ice and the mysteries of the animal kingdom.
We marvel at what a great God he is and to be praised.
Thank him for being open for business day and night.

Ponder: As a child of God,
prayer is kind of like
calling home everyday.

Today I am grateful for

Ponder Time

Be the light

What Can I Do

A partner can have many meanings to
people. It could be a colleague, comrade,
friend, consort, associate, companion, mate
or participant. Jesus gave many examples while on
earth and he especially mentioned you are my friend.
"I lay down my life for my friends." He also mentioned he
was the bridegroom and would come again for his bride
(the church.) He is a constant companion as he said,
"I am with you always even unto the end."
As a comrade he helps us fight our battles with Satan.
A friend is someone you are close to and you like to do
things together in work or recreation. A close friend is
one you can share your most intimate thoughts with that
you wouldn't discuss with others.
Our God is a mighty God, but extraordinarily, God waits on
human partners to work with him to achieve his purposes.
He is the power and wisdom behind us.
All things are possible with this kind of partner.
He is waiting to be asked.
"What can I do?"

A sweet friendship refreshes the soul. Proverbs 27:9

Ponder: You may be only one person in the world,
but you may also be the world to one person.

Today I am grateful for

Become the Change

Ponder Time

_____

_____

_____

_____

_____

_____

_____

_____

_____

_____

_____

Be the light

Grace and Glory

We sing the song, "Amazing Grace" quite
often. Do we really understand the meaning of
grace? It is God unconditionally favoring us with
nothing we have done to deserve it. We were
born in sin and that is what separates us from God.
But he loved us so much he sent his son Jesus to die
on the cross for our sins.
Grace is God's riches at Christ's expense.
Our part is to accept the salvation offered us. Even though
we can't be perfect, his grace is sufficient for us.
He helps us to stay on the right path.
"So then carry the cross patiently and with perfect
submission, and in the end the cross will carry you."
(Thomas Kempis)
If you live close to God and his infinite grace,
you don't have to tell, it shows on your face.

2nd Timothy 1:9 It is he who saved us and chose us for his
holy work, not because we deserved it but because that was
his plan long before the world began–to show his love and
kindness to us through Christ.

Psalm 86:11 For Jehovah God is our Light and Protector.
He gives us grace and glory.
No good thing will he withhold from those who
walk along his path.

Today I am grateful for

Let's make today beautiful

Ponder Time

Be the light

The Net to Catch Us

We are putting more and more emphasis
on safety in our daily lives. Circus performers
use a safety net even when they are very
experienced. Firemen hold a net for people to
jump out of windows. Utility workers use a bucket
in a crane to reach high places otherwise it is too
dangerous to try and work there. Window washers have a
safety harness besides the scaffolding.
One of the first questions asked after a car accident is,
"Were they wearing a seat belt?" Helmets are needed for
motorcycle and bicycle riders.
More and more precautions are taken for our own safety
that we didn't use to give much thought to.
One of the reasons is because lawsuits are more common
if the companies don't provide for the workers' safety.
People are quick to blame someone else even if they
might have been careless themselves.
If we put so much emphasis on our concern for our
earthly life, then why don't we make sure
we are secured for eternity?
God has provided all the necessary steps for our security.
Jesus is the net to catch us. Why take a chance?

The last act of Jesus was to save a soul.

Ponder: He who dies with the most toys is still dead.

Today I am grateful for

Believe in Yourself

Ponder This

Be the light

Wake Up Call

We hear the words, "wake up call," in the news
very often these days. It is not your usual thinking
of getting up in the morning. Rather it is said after a
tragedy or a bad situation has occurred.
Election reform, power outage in California, school shootings,
Firestone tire separation, faulty childrens' car seats and cribs, oil
spills and rising heating bills are just some of the wake up calls.
Most of these are not our responsibility but they
do affect us in many ways.
The companies that are responsible are made to recall the
product or correct the situation. They, of course, stand by their
product until forced to confess their errors.
Many are not easily solved.
We sort of go on day by day complaining about the situations
and rely on higher authorities. But sometimes the wake up call
can be a danger signal to us of chest pain, the word cancer,
fires, diseases in animals, overseas etc. When these danger
signals appear it gets our attention immediately. We put off our
hereafter, thinking it just happens to someone else.
But our demise can be at any time and is a wake up call to the
question, "Where do you plan to go after you die?"
Jesus died on the cross for our sins. Believing in Him and
asking Him to come into your heart is the answer to your
wake up call for eternity. Don't put it off.

The Lord your God…is always with you. He celebrates and sings
because of you, and He will refresh your life with His love.
Zephaniah 3:17

Today I am grateful for

Ponder Time

Be the light

Our Daily Report Card

The school year is about over and it's
report card time. Nine months have gone by
fast but the report card tells the final results
whether you pass or fail. Even little children get
attendance, effort, conduct and citizenship reports to
let them know how they rate.
Does God have a daily report card going for us? In the past
nine months how would you score? Did you attend Church
regularly, pray, tithe, serve God and others? Did you put forth
all the effort you could or did you do a haphazardly job?
God knows your thoughts and deeds whether you've been
naughty or nice, if you lied or cheated or worse.
Someday our life will be revealed to us on God's standards.
How will our accomplishments be recorded? Maybe now is
a good time to take stock of our lives and improve on our
failures. God is willing to help us if we ask.

Ask, and you will be given what you ask for. Seek, and you
will find. Knock, and the door will be opened. For everyone
who asks, receives. Anyone who seeks, finds.
If only you will knock, the door will open. Matthew 7:7

Ponder: There is no key to happiness.
The door is always open.

Today I am grateful for

Shine bright

Ponder Time

_____

_____

_____

_____

_____

_____

_____

_____

_____

_____

_____

Be the light

One of A Kind

Your brain is very small compared to the
rest of your body, but it controls everything.
If you watch any of the game shows, the trivia
they ask can go way back in the recess of your brain
to something even in your childhood. You probably haven't
thought about it for years until the subject came up and it
triggered a memory. You wonder how all this information
can be stored for years in such a compact area.
The brain does not rest during sleep. It stays quite active.
Sleep experts say that during sleep, the brain is sorting out
information it took during the day and filing it for future
retrieval. No wonder we wake up tired and groggy if we
don't get enough sleep.
Besides storing information and recalling it on command,
our brain is constantly sending signals to other parts of our
body to fulfill their duties. It seems so overwhelming we say,
"It boggles my mind to think about it."
Your brain is one organ that cannot be replaced.
Praise God for creating you in his image because you are
wonderfully made. Your brain is one of a kind.
No one else has the same brain, fingerprints or D.N.A.

His divine power has given us everything we need for life
and godliness through our knowledge of Him who called us
by His own glory and goodness. 2nd Peter 1:3

Today I am grateful for

Ponder Time

Be the light

Our Spiritual Pulse

This summer has been extremely hot
and the heat index makes it even hotter. The heat
index is compared to the chill factor when we had
freezing midwest weather last winter. The RAGBRAI
bicyclists said the wind was worse than the heat one day.
Our body temperature can go up or down, too.
A visit to the doctor includes your temperature and
blood pressure checks.
Do we have a spiritual temperature? If God took your
spiritual pulse, what would it read? Oftentimes we neglect
our physical health until a crisis appears and then
we have a rise in our spiritual temperature.
God says in Revelation 3:15-16, "I know your works. You
are neither hot nor cold: I wish you were one or the other!
But since you are merely lukewarm,
I will spit you out of my mouth!"
We have choices everyday to seek God in nature, in
people, in His word or prayer. More than likely we would
rank a low spiritual pulse. We spend time doing a physical
workout but we also need to spend time doing
spiritual work for the Lord. You will be blessed.

May you be blessed by the Lord,
the maker of heaven and earth. Psalm 115:15

The Lord bless you and keep you. Numbers 6:24

Today I am grateful for

All THINGS are POSSIBLE

Ponder Time

_____
_____
_____
_____
_____
_____
_____
_____
_____
_____
_____

Be the light

We All Live Under The Same Sun

Almost every time we purchase something it has a barcode or price sticker to show how much it is worth. Sometimes the same item can be found at a cheaper price at a discount store or even go on sale for specials.

Do we have a barcode in God's eyes to show how much we are worth? Are professional people worth much more than poorer people?

Black markets sell babies, children, innocent girls and laborers as if life had no value but greed to the sellers to make a profit. These people's lives are destroyed even if they are ever set free.

In God's eyes we are all equal regardless of race or creed. St. Therese says, "The sun shines equally on cedars and every tiny flower. In just the same way God looks after every soul as if it had no equal. All is planned for the good of every soul, exactly as the seasons are so arranged that the humblest daisy blooms at the appointed time."

We are all made in God's image.

"How great is the love the Father has lavished on us, that we should be called children of God! And that is what we are!" 1 John 3:1

Ponder: Birthdays are good for you: the more you have the longer you live.

Today I am grateful for

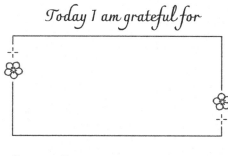

Choose Peace

Ponder Time

Be the light

Too Soon–Too Late

When the first Pilgrims came to our shores
they were greeted by the people they called
"Indians," with offers of friendship. They freely
shared their food and shelter with them. Many of
the Pilgrims wouldn't have survived without their
help so they were extremely thankful.
Since the terrorist attacks on September 11, our world has
drastically changed. We were a nation concerned with our
own selves, but everyone has taken stock of their families
and concern for others since.
There has been an outpouring of patriotism, giving blood,
prayers, sympathy and donations of all kinds. Even children
have made cards, collected stuffed bears, made homemade
angels to hang for Christmas and much more to show support
for our country and families that have lost loved ones.
Since the first Thanksgiving history has not been kind to the
Indians. Our government has not lived up to its promise.
Despite their poverty the Indians are not bitter and have done
bake sales, mainly Indian tacos, a taco made with Indian
fry bread, to reach out to the victims of these tragedies
in other parts of our country.
Some are on active military duty or on call.
We are all trying to make a difference in our lives and any
small way helps us to be united and be thankful to God for
each new day, our neighbors and those who work
to keep us safe.

Ponder: You can never do an act of kindness too soon,
for you never know how soon it will be too late.

November 2001   41

Today I am grateful for

you are
AMAZING

Ponder Time

Be the light
✿✿

Prince of Peace

We often suffer but we are never crushed.
Even when we don't know what to do, we never give up.
In times of trouble, God is with us, and when we are
knocked down, we get up again.
2 Corinthians 4: 8-9
These verses sum up the unity displayed by our country
after the September 11 attack. Instead of dividing America,
we have discovered it has done just the opposite. It has
brought Americans closer than ever before. It has unified the
entire world to a degree never before dreamed possible.
One thing we have learned is we can't change the past and
today is what counts. Material things are not nearly as
important as staying in touch with loved ones and friends,
letting them know we are thinking about them.
More people are connecting with God, and doing good will
because tomorrow is uncertain. Jesus set an example by
his humble birth and desire to bring peace. This is what
he wants us to do, to trust him, fear not, and settle any
differences we have with others.
He is the Prince of Peace.
The world needs it now more than ever.

Ponder: A grudge is a heavy thing to carry.

Today I am grateful for

THE LORD IS MY
Light
AND
Salvation

PSALM 27:1

Ponder Time

Be the light

Duty Calls

When a servant comes in from plowing or
taking care of sheep, he just doesn't sit down
and eat, but first prepares his master's meal and
serves him his supper before he eats his own.
And he is not even thanked, for he is merely doing what
he is supposed to do. Just so, if you merely obey me,
you should not consider yourselves worthy of praise.
For you have simply done your duty. Luke 17:7-10
Just what is our duty to the Lord? Going about our normal
lives often is for our own pleasure.
God expects us to obey him and serve him.
What we do is just part of our duty to the Lord in
serving him and others and we shouldn't expect glory.
We like to be acknowledged when we have done a good
job, but the real credit goes to God for giving us the talents
and abilities to perform our duties.
Jesus was a servant to man and set a good example.

Ecclesiastes 12: 13-14, Here is my final conclusion: fear
God and obey his commandments, for this is the entire duty
of man. For God will judge us for everything we do,
including every hidden thing, good or bad.
Start the new year right by fearing God and obeying him.

Ponder: Dear God, I have a problem, it's Me.

Today I am grateful for

Ponder Time

Be the light

Starting Your Heart

The heart is the most vital organ of the body. It supplies blood to all the rest of the body. Even if the brain is declared legally dead the heart can still beat. But the heart is more than an organ to supply life, it is the root of all our emotions. Hatred, revenge, evil acts and any sin starts in the heart. They can get out of control and road rage, sports rage, envy, anger, and jealousy can lead to murders and destruction.

On the flip side of the coin, love can start in the heart and do all kinds of good deeds. More and more people are going out of their way to go the extra mile to show their love and concern especially since the terrorists' attacks. Those who give and those who receive have a feeling of joy.

Many of today's health problems can be related to the emotional stress put on the heart and brain from heated arguments, long sufferings from abuse, etc. But those who show love are prone to live more healthy and peaceful lives. So why do people instill hatred in their society when love can be so much more beneficial?

God is love and we are made in his image so he expects us to love.

Great is His unfailing LOVE. Lamentations 3:32
Enjoy abundant blessings from His heart to you!

I have you in my heart. Philippians 1:7

Today I am grateful for

Become the Change

Ponder Time

_____
_____
_____
_____
_____
_____
_____
_____
_____
_____
_____
_____

Be the light

Life's a Bed of Roses

The old adage, "Life Is Just a Bed of Roses," is so true. Roses are beautiful to watch as they unfold and their fragrance fills the air. But you'll also find out most roses have thorns along the stems if you go to pick them.

Life is like that, some days are rosy and beautiful and you enjoy them to the fullest. Other days everything goes wrong; an illness, accident, death, divorce, loss of a job, etc.

We must remember Christ's life was not a bed of roses for him either. Some days were spent healing the sick, feeding large crowds, teaching God's word and life seemed full. On the down side his hometown people knew him as a carpenter's son and couldn't accept him as the Messiah. In one short week he was betrayed by one of his disciples and denied by another. He was rejected, scorned, beaten and crucified. A crown of thorns was placed on his head and they were very real and painful.

If we need to complain about our life and want to blame it on God, we only need to look at Christ's life. He was without sin and in only three years of ministry his days could be up or down yet he accepted the thorns in his life for our sake.

Love is patient, kind, it bears all things, believes all things, hopes all things, endures all things.
Love never ends. 1 Corinthians 13

Ponder: Love doesn't make the world go 'round.
Love is what makes the ride worthwhile. Franklin P. Jones

Today I am grateful for

Let's make TODAY beautiful

Ponder Time

Be the light
✿✿✿

Spreading His Word

When Jesus was born, the first ones
to see the new baby were the shepherds.
They were considered a lowly cast of people
who spent a great deal of time just tending their flocks.
Their education was on the job training.
Easter morning the first ones at the tomb were the
women. They were taking spices to anoint his body but
found the tomb empty and Jesus had risen from the dead.
Women didn't rank very high on the social ladder.
It was the men who were the authoritative figures and
kept the women in the background and taken for granted.
So where were the men? Why didn't they go to the tomb
early? They were hiding and teary eyed thinking they might
be the next ones killed because they were his disciples.
Jesus appeared to the disciples to prove he was alive.
His message is, "Go ye therefore and make disciples in
all the world, obey all the commands. I am with you
always even unto the end of the world."
Jesus didn't discriminate against race, color, creed
or social rank. He died for all so our job is to be teaching
and spreading his word all over the earth.
You reveal the path of life to me;
in Your presence is abundant joy. Psalm 16:11

Ponder: God is using you to touch your world
—one person at a time.

Today I am grateful for

Believe in Yourself

Ponder This

Be the light
✿✿✿

Celebrate the Church's Birthday

Pentecost means 50th and the Jews celebrated this annually. It was fifty days after the Passover ceremonies when Christ was crucified. As the believers met that day, suddenly there was a sound like the roaring of a mighty windstorm in the skies above them and it filled the house where they were meeting. Then, what looked like flames or tongues of fire appeared and settled on their heads. Everyone present was filled with the Holy Spirit and began speaking in languages they didn't know, for the Holy Spirit gave them this ability.

This was the birthday of the church. Peter preached a long sermon and those who believed were baptized, about 3,000 in all. They joined with others in regular attendance, in communion, services, prayer meetings and worship together. A stick by itself can easily be broken, but tied together in a bundle it has great strength. This is why it is so important that God wants us to gather together to worship, share in joy and sorrow with one another and gain strength in numbers as Christians.

The people meeting on that first day were from neighboring lands and even visitors from Rome.

Each was telling about the mighty miracles of God in their own language. We are commanded to do likewise.

Whoever serves Me must follow Me; and where I am, My servant also will be. My Father will honor the one who serves Me. John 12:26

Ponder: The way you serve others is such a beautiful reflection of our Saviour's love.

Today I am grateful for

Ponder Time

BE KIND

Be the light

A Different View

A family moved into a new community and started
attending a new church. The front of the church was
adorned with a huge hand crafted wooden cross.
At an evening service they were about to attend, the six year old
son excitedly asked, "Do I go downstairs or do I get to stay in
the 'big plus' room?"
Have you ever thought of the cross as being a plus in your life?
It definitely isn't a minus. Many times your blessings even multiply.
More and more jobs now have perks or added benefits such as
paid vacation, sick leave, health insurance, retirement plan,
stock in the company, etc.
What are the added benefits or perks of being a Christian?
The most important is by accepting Jesus you are assured a ticket
to heaven. There is also more love, more grace, more mercy and
more peace than we could hope for. There are answered prayers.
By praying it brings power to do what we couldn't do on our own.
We have a sense of calmness and inner peace.
People who turn to God for guidance and day to day living,
live longer and have fewer health problems.
The little boy was right, the cross is a "big plus" in our lives.
Sometimes it takes a child to lead us in a different view and
see things in a new light.

Ponder: A couple was celebrating their seventy-fifth wedding
anniversary, and this old gentleman, past ninety, was asked
why he was still so healthy. "Well," he said, "whenever ma and me
had a disagreement, I decided that rather than argue it out to the
bitter end, I would put on my hat and go for a walk. I guess I'm
healthy "cause I have spent a good part of my life in the open air."

Today I am grateful for

Shine bright

Ponder Time

Be the light

Be Still and Listen

A saying you may have heard is, "We cannot control the wind but we can adjust our sails."
Bad things happen to us all the time but how we react to the situation is in our hands.
If you remember Elijah heard the whirlwind, the earthquake and the fire. God was not in any of those but when it calmed down Elijah heard God's voice telling him what to do.
A whirlwind has swept through our church and now that the wind has settled we need to hear God's voice for our future.
Perhaps we need to change an attitude, volunteer more, pray and support one another.
We all need a break or time out in our daily routines. If we really want to know the vision for our future we need to be still and listen to that voice telling us what we can do to adjust our sails. Then we can get back on course.
Be still and know that I am God,
I am exalted among the nations,
I am exalted in the earth!
Psalms 46:10

Ponder: We could learn a lot from crayons: some are sharp, some are pretty, some are dull, some have weird names, and all are different colors...but they all have to learn to live in the same box.

Today I am grateful for

Ponder Time

Be the light

The Boomerang Effect

A boomerang is an Australian club designed to throw so that it comes back very near you. It's also an act of utterance that backfires on its originator. The Bible has numerous examples of people doing this. Peter denied Christ and he wept bitterly. Judas betrayed him and later committed suicide. Our modern day economy is in a slump largely due to corporate greed, power and fraud. They deny wrongdoing but now their sins are being made public and they should be punished. They don't think of all the working people they have left without jobs or security. We are not guilty of scandals like this but our tongue and actions can get us into trouble and come back to haunt us and make us feel guilty. We all have said angry or hurtful words on a spur of the moment. We cannot take back words but they are not easily forgotten. "Whatever is in the heart overflows into speech." Luke 6:45 It displeases the Lord to see his people do these things. "Try to show as much compassion as your Father does. Never criticize or condemn- or it will all come back on you. Go easy on others; then they will do the same for you." Luke 6:36-37 It is better to show love and have love return back to you.

Ponder: Those who wait to give something to the poor until they are wealthy themselves, will never give. (Chinese Proverb)

Today I am grateful for

All THINGS are POSSIBLE

Ponder Time

Be the light
✿✿✿

Who's Your
Power Source

Everything nowadays is so automatic
we think we can't get along without it. Our cars,
kitchen appliances, faxes, telephones, airplanes
can go on autopilot, etc.
What do we do with all of our so-called free time?
We hurry on to something else. We become lazy and
complacent. We can get along with all of the modern
equipment until there is a power shortage.
Do we think God is automatic and can be tuned in and out
on our command? We are not automatically forgiven, healed
or blessed just because we are good people. God is the
power source and supreme being we will be accountable to.
We are all sinners and need to ask for forgiveness.
If our prayer lists are all selfish then they probably won't get
answered. We need to set aside all the distractions of this
world and come to God in solitude. He expects us to greet
him in praise and thanksgiving before we begin making
requests. If we come in a humble spirit he will hear our
secrets. "Seek the Lord, all you humble of the land, you who
do what he commands. Seek righteousness, seek humility;
perhaps you will be sheltered on the day of the Lord's anger."
Zephaniah 2:3
Whatever you do, work at it with all your heart,
as working for the Lord, not for men, since you know that
you will receive an inheritance from the Lord as a reward.
It is the Lord Christ you are serving. Colossians 3:23-24

Today I am grateful for

Choose Peace

Ponder Time

62

Be the light

What is So Important

A young boy went to visit his friend. When it was time to eat a meal the boy was waiting for them to say grace. When they didn't he said, "You people are just like my dog, you start right in." Are we so ungrateful that we can't give God thanks for our daily needs? Think of all the people the world over that are in desperate need. Many can't survive from day to day. It has been said the average Christian spends 3 minutes a day in prayer to God and the clergy 7 minutes. That's not very long out of a 24 hour day. So what is our excuse that everything else is more important? We can talk at length to friends or family on the phone or just visit. Then why is it so difficult when God already knows every detail about us but is waiting patiently to hear from us in return?

"O, come, let us sing to the Lord! Give a joyous shout in honor of the Rock of our salvation. Come before him with thankful hearts. Let us sing him psalms of praise. For the Lord God is a great God, the great King of all Gods."
Psalms 95:1-3

"Give thanks in all circumstances, for this is God's will for you in Christ Jesus."
1 Thessalonians 5:18

Ponder: " Most of us go to our grave with our music still inside of us unplayed."
-Oliver Wendell Holmes.

Today I am grateful for

you are
AMAZING

Ponder Time

Be the light
✿✿✿

Making a U-Turn
Right

When Mary and Joseph arrived at the inn
they were turned away. Then they were humbled
to find refuge in a stable. Instead of returning later to
Nazareth they were turned away to flee to Egypt.
Jesus' life has been one of rejection.
People couldn't believe he was the Messiah. Angry mobs
had him crucified and his disciples had turned away from him
in fear of their own lives. Yet Jesus didn't turn away from the
sick, the blind, the poor and the downcast.
How often do we turn away from God? We do whatever we
want and spend our money on whatever we want, yet
God loves us and continues to bless us.
We can make a U-turn in our lives and turn to God instead
of turning away. Some day we will give an accounting of our
actions and God may turn away from us.
Let us remember what Christmas is all about. God loved us
so much that He sent his Son so we might have salvation.
Don't turn away from Him but come to the
Prince of Peace.

Ponder: A truly happy person is one who can enjoy the
scenery on a detour.

Today I am grateful for

THE LORD IS MY
Light
AND
Salvation

PSALM 27:1

Ponder Time

Be the light

What's Your Bottom Line

A common phrase people in all walks of life are using today states, "The Bottom Line Is....." It might mean; no tax increase, lowest price we can offer, if you can benefit from the injection take it, take it or leave it, tell the truth or suffer the consequences, it's been questioned before, it requires a small effort on your part that pays off big, it boils down to racism, they have no control and no accountability, same thing will happen again, money back guarantee, saves time, etc. Don't these answers sound very familiar? Some are an evasive answer to a question that gives you a false impression.

In this day and age we often lack the faith to trust their judgment in matters we can't control.

The only person we can trust is God.

He knows our day by day needs.

Psalms 118:8 It is better to trust the Lord than to put confidence in men. It is better to take refuge in him than the mightiest king!
Jeremiah 17:5 The Lord says: cursed is the man who puts his trust in mortal man and turns his heart away from God.

Ponder: If a hypocrite is standing between you and God, the hypocrite is closer to God than you are.

Today I am grateful for

Ponder Time

Be the light
✫✫✫✫✫

Fulfill Your Purpose

Recently a high school teacher asked
the class what their purpose in life was.
Some of the youth gave flippant answers, but
one girl said, "To be nice to people."
The teacher said, "Good answer."
Two thousand years ago the people were disobedient to
God and so he sent his son, Jesus, to die on the cross to
save us. That was his main purpose for coming,
so we could have eternal life.
Matthew 3:24-25 states,
"A kingdom divided against itself will collapse.
A home filled with strife and division destroys itself."
Abraham Lincoln said the same thing.
A house divided against itself will fall.
The church is God's home and we are all God's children.
So now we ask, "What is our purpose in life?" We are put
here in Winthrop, Iowa for a reason. We could have been
born in Iraq or North Korea or some other country
but God has a mission for us here.
Let us seek God's plan for our future and follow his
direction so it can be fulfilled.

"And we know that in all things God works for the good of
those who love him, who have been called
according to his purpose." Romans 8:28

Ponder: The most important things in your house
are the people.

Today I am grateful for

Become the Change

Ponder Time

_____
_____
_____
_____
_____
_____
_____
_____
_____
_____
_____

Be the light
✿✿✿✿

Where's Your Focus

At age 30, Jesus was baptized by John in the Jordan River. The moment he came up out of the water, he saw the heavens open and the Holy Spirit, in the form of a dove, descending on him and a voice from heaven said, "You are my beloved Son, you are my Delight." This is the only time the complete Trinity is recorded. What a pinnacle of his life this must have been for Jesus. You would think with this high Jesus would start his ministry. But, no, God had other plans. Immediately the Holy Spirit urged Jesus into the desert. There for forty days, alone except for the desert animals, he was subjected to Satan's temptations to sin. And afterwards the angels came and cared for him.

Imagine being alone in a desert for a month and a third. We couldn't stand to be alone very long without communication. This was God's way of preparing him for the ministry, even being tempted by Satan. Jesus was to be wholly dependent on God.

When we are under pressure our focus is on the matter on hand. But when we relax we let our guard down and become vulnerable. This is when Satan loves to tempt us into sin and we can easily fail.

Jesus overcame Satan's temptations by quoting Scripture. When we are being led astray we need to call on God to be of good courage and strength to overcome the evil. And he said unto me, "My grace is sufficient for thee; for my strength is made perfect in weakness." 2 Corinthians 12:9

Today I am grateful for

Ponder Time

Be the light
✿✿✿✿✿

A Meeting or
A Message

Most of us attend meeting after meeting of some sort. There is usually an agenda and not always do the participants agree on everything. A meeting can be very short, or drag on, until it is adjourned.

A social gathering is an entirely different atmosphere. One is in a lighter mood and enjoys the friendship. There is usually some food to share. Think of all the family gatherings, sports events, movies, etc. where we get together to bond.

Such was the Last Supper Jesus shared with his friends. It was not a meeting but a gathering around the table sharing bread and wine. This has been recorded as a very special time and as often as we celebrate it we remember that Jesus died for us.

These special gatherings shared around food and fellowship are the things we remember, too.

That's probably why Jesus didn't call it a meeting, even though he had a message to tell everyone, but is to be remembered as the Last Supper.

Ponder: Silence is often misinterpreted but never misquoted.

Today I am grateful for

Believe
in
Yourself

Ponder This

Be the light
✿✿✿✿✿

Growing Together

The oldest living things on earth are the giant
redwoods (sequoias) in California. Ponder the fact that
while some of these trees swayed as saplings, on the
other side of the world Christ was born.
When Columbus discovered America in 1492 the same
trees had grown to towering heights. So the average age of
the tree is between 2000 to 3000 years old.
These trees can grow up to 250 to 300 feet and the diameter
at the base is 30 to 40 feet.
The trees stand alone in the world...there are no other trees
anywhere like the giant sequoias. The remarkable feature about
the redwood is its resistance to disease and fire. This is due to
the thick bark, the small amount of resin and the sponge-like
quality of the wood which absorbs water easily.
We can learn a lesson from these giants. The roots spread
40 to 50 feet from the base of the tree at about 4 to 6 feet below
the surface. To support the tree the roots grow together.
Every part of the tree serves a definite purpose to make it sturdy.
The trees grow straight up, true and fine,
as they look up to the one who created them.
We can pattern our lives like these trees also. We gain strength
when we support one another, when our life is running straight and
true and when we look up to lofty heights to
worship our creator.

"Our bodies have many parts, but the many parts make up only
one body when they are all put together. So it is with the 'body' of
Christ. Each of us is a part of the one body of Christ."
1 Corinthians 12:12-13

Today I am grateful for

Ponder Time

BE KIND

Be the light
✦✦✦✦

Pieces of Glass

Strangers have commented on what a pretty
church we have. Probably the leading feature is
the stained glass windows.
Many churches have windows that are intricately laid with
many pieces of colored glass. Stained glass has served as
both decoration and architecture for centuries.
In ancient times when people could not read or write, the
windows could tell a story and a message from the Bible and
be handed down from generation to generation.
The windows really illuminate the stories when the
sunlight shines through them.
They illuminate the hearts and minds of people
to give glory to God's name.
We are the church, too, and make up many parts
just like the pieces of the windows.

Matthew 5:16 tells it best. "Let your light shine before men,
so that they can see your good works and
give glory to your
Father who is in heaven."

Love…is the perfect bond of unity. Colossians 3:14

Ponder: If you worry, you didn't pray.
If you pray, don't worry.

Today I am grateful for

shine bright

Ponder Time

Be the light

Living in a Perfect World

Rodney Dangerfield, a comedian, always had his by-line, "I Got No Respect." For years his monologue was on various situations but the same theme. He even got no respect from his dog.
People laughed at his jokes but there was an underlying thought of truth.
How often do we fail to respect another person's opinion or call them names? Verbal abuse causes hurt feelings and anger. We respect our own privacy, careful drivers, care of our property and the environment and we should respect theirs as well.
Young people are trashing and bullying up on others so young. They give no heed to a mob mentality and someone gets hurt or killed. Adults are not setting a good example in the home environment and beyond.
More and more we are finding people polluting the streams, rivers and the air until they are unsafe for drinking or to breathe. This is not what God intended when he made a perfect world. We try to blame someone else but we are guilty of being rude, impolite or a don't care attitude.

The Golden Rule is "Do unto others
as you would have them
do unto you."
Show respect.

Ponder: Always forgive your enemies,
nothing annoys them so much.

Today I am grateful for

TRUST THE TIMING OF YOUR LIFE

Ponder Time

Be the light
✿✿✿✿✿

Children Are Our Future

A teacher has a plaque that reads:
"Children may be half our size,
but they are all of our future."
God loves children and he emphasized it
many times in the Bible.
"Children are a gift from the Lord." Psalms 127:3
A familiar one is, "Jesus took the children in his arms,
placed his hands on each of them and blessed them."
Mark 10:16
Teach children how they should live,
and they will remember it all their life. Proverbs 22:6
We are all God's children no matter what our age.
That's why we call him Father. "Since you are God's dear
children, you must try to be like him." Ephesians 5:1
"As a father is kind to his children, so the Lord is kind to
those who honor him." Psalms 103:13
"See how much the Father has loved us! His love is so
great that we are called God's children." 1 John 3:1a
Remember you are loved at any age. Even if you were
the only child of God he would love you very much.
That's why He sent his son to die on the cross for you.

Satisfy us in the morning with your unfailing love that we
may sing for joy and be glad all our days. Psalms 90:14

Ponder: How long a minute is depends on which side
of the bathroom door you're on.

Today I am grateful for

Ponder Time

All THINGS are POSSIBLE

Be the light
☆☆☆☆☆

Two Sides of a Coin

When we were growing up and had done
something bad we probably heard, "You should be
ashamed of yourself." History repeats itself and we
say the same thing to our children.
God was ashamed of his rebellious children and they were
punished for it. Moses and the Israelites wandered in the
desert for 40 years because they worshiped idols. Jonah
refused God's command and was in the stomach of the
whale for 3 days. The list goes on and is even worse today.
Look at the mess the world is in.
A coin has two sides and so does being ashamed. Are we
ashamed of God and put other things first? People take his
name in vain, lie to cover up wrong deeds, cheat, are
unfaithful, fail to speak up for Christ and that is
just the beginning.
Where does all of this end? Christ explains it in Mark 8:38.
"If a person is ashamed of me and my message in these
adulterous and sinful days, I, the Son of Man, will be
ashamed of that person when I return in the glory of my
Father with the holy angels."

A black ant on black marble in a dark night! God sees it.
(Arab proverb)

Today I am grateful for

Choose Peace

Ponder Time

Be the light
✿✿✿✿✿

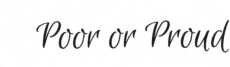

Poor or Proud

For over the past year the news media has been
reporting the corporate greed of many companies.
After they have been caught, bankruptcies have occurred,
leaving many employees out of jobs and their pensions depleted
plus stockholders in failure. They have even set their own rules for
benefits and perks. Some have destroyed documents to cover up
their greed, which is an obstruction of justice.
Recently the C.E.O of the New York Stock Exchange was forced
to resign over his lavish $187.5 million pay package.
Have these people no concern for their excessive greed and
possessions than to put the lives of so many people at risk just for
their own selfish gain?
They should have realized the scandal that would result if caught
and the fall from grace for them or their families and all
those who trusted them.
Proverbs 15:27 states: "He who is greedy for unjust gain makes
trouble for his household, but he who hates bribes will live."
Proverbs 16:8, "A little gained honesty is better than great wealth
gotten by dishonest means."
Proverbs 6:11, "The Lord demands fairness in every business deal.
He established this principle.
"It is better to be poor and humble than proud and rich."
Proverbs 16:19
Psalms 107:1, "Say "Thank you to the Lord for being so good,
for always being so loving and kind."

Ponder: Do the math…count your blessings.

Today I am grateful for

you are
AMAZING

Ponder Time

Be the light
✿✿✿✿

The Morning and Evening Star

We rate people and things with stars, examples;
4 star generals, 5 star cars, hotels, restaurants, and
a star on the Hollywood Walk of Fame.
Even children get stars for good grades and performances.
Yet none of these can compare to Jesus' special star the
shepherds and the wise men followed in search of Jesus'
birth. Not only were the stars brilliant but the angels were
announcing his birth as well.
He did not have an ambulance nor a first class hospital but
a humble manger. His parents were lowly citizens and the
media was not aware to publish the good news. Even if they
did, he was not ranked noteworthy at the time.
But now the whole world knows about his birth,
life, death, and resurrection.
He is the Morning Star and the Evening Star.
People spend months planning for weddings, celebrations,
trips, etc. but there was no exact advance notice, only
prophecies. No baby shower either and then they were told
to flee the country.
God's plan for Jesus' birth was to let people know he came
as a Savior for all ranks of people from the lowliest on up.
There is no distinction in his sight. God certainly works in
mysterious ways. Praise the Lord!

Ponder: A tiny bouquet of flowers can fill a room with
sunshine; a little act of kindness can fill a heart with joy.

Today I am grateful for

THE LORD IS MY
Light
AND
Salvation

PSALM 27:1

Ponder Time

Be the light

Snow that Sparkles

What kind of purification system does God have that he can turn all the grimy, dirty water we create into pure white snow?

When a few inches of snow falls it makes all kinds of interesting shapes and forms. The sun sparkles on it and makes it glisten. It's so bright you need dark glasses. That can change rapidly when we start moving it and driving on it. Then it gets mushy and splatters all over. But God can clean up the mess and send us another batch of pure white snow.

The Bible also tells us that our sins are filthy to him. When we ask for forgiveness we can be cleansed as white as the snow.

Isaiah 1:18 states, "Come, let's talk this over! says the Lord: no matter how deep the stains of your sins are, I can take it out and make you as clean as freshly fallen snow. Even if you are stained as red as crimson, I can make you white as wool."

Praise God for his purification system with nature and with us.

Ponder: The three biggest reasons for going to a warmer climate: December, January and February.

Today I am grateful for

Ponder Time

Be the light
✿✿✿✿✿✿

Promises Kept

The media is full of ads of presidential candidates pursuing their promises of what they intend to do if elected. Then at the closing each will say, "I approve this message." They also tell us we have the power to elect them and our country will be changed.

These hopefuls, if elected, can only serve 8 years at the most and won't be able to keep their promises because they have lots more people in the governing process to approve them.

Jesus never ran for an office but he is the message. He keeps his promises and doesn't need human approval of his deeds. He made the supreme sacrifice for our sins. That's why God sent Jesus as the messenger to proclaim the Good News that God is love and we can believe what his word tells us in the Bible.

The source of power is in God's hands, not ours.

God can change our lives if we put our trust in him.

1st John 4:16-17 We know how much God loves us, and we have put our trust in him. God is love, and all who live in love, live in God, and God lives in them. And as we live in God, our love grows more perfect.

Seek God's will in all you do, and He will show you the path to take. Proverbs 3:6

Today I am grateful for

Become the Change

Ponder Time

_____
_____
_____
_____
_____
_____
_____
_____
_____
_____
_____

Be the light
☆☆☆☆☆

Proof of Ownership

Years ago ranchers branded their cattle with a hot branding iron with their farm initials or logo to identify them from cattle rustlers. This seemed so cruel but was necessary to prove ownership. It caused the animal suffering and it left a permanent scar. Today ear tags are commonly used but they still can be lost or removed.

Jesus has proof of his ownership over each of us. At his crucifixion his hands were nailed to the cross. It is even recorded in the Old Testament years before Jesus was born. Isaiah 49: 15-16 tells us, "Does a woman forget her baby at the breast, or fail to cherish the son of her womb? Yet even if they forget, I will never forget you. See, I have branded you on the palm of your hands."

His suffering on the cross was very cruel but he did it willingly so we could have permanent residency in Heaven if we believe and accept him as our Savior.

He tends His flock like a shepherd: He gathers the lambs in His arms and carries them close to His heart. Isaiah 40:11

Today I am grateful for

Ponder Time

Be the light
☆☆☆☆☆

The Task of Painting

This is the time of the Easter season and it
reminds us of Leonardo da Vinci's painting of
The Last Supper.
It is told that when he was working on the picture he was
angry with a certain man. He said bitter words and made
threats to him. When he returned to the task of painting the
face of Jesus he was unable to do so. Finally he put down his
equipment and sought the man to ask for his forgiveness.
The man accepted his apology. Leonardo returned to his
workshop and was able to complete the face of Jesus.
One of the last words Jesus uttered on the cross was,
"Father, forgive them for they know not what they do."
Jesus was without sin but was beaten, rejected, spit upon,
jeered and was brutally crucified on the cross but yet
he was able to forgive.
Anger can cause us to do things we would regret later.
Harboring anger does more ill will to one's self than the other
person. By forgiving, the burden is lifted and you are set free.
Colossians 3:13 states "You must make allowances for
each other's faults and forgive the person who offends you.
Remember the Lord forgives you,
so you must forgive others."

Ponder: "True creativity often starts where language ends."
Arthur Koestler

Today I am grateful for

Believe
in
Yourself

Ponder This

Be the light

The Missed Opportunity

In 1892 the Queen of England liked to disguise herself and walk among the cottages of the poor.
One day the Queen was caught in a shower and stopped at a dwelling of an old woman.
She asked if she had an umbrella to lend her.
The old woman did not recognize the Queen.
The old woman granted the request grudgingly. She told her she had two umbrellas, one was good and the other an old one. The dame replied, "You can take this one. I guess I'll never see it again."
She gave the royal lady the one with the whale ribs seen here and there through the coarse torn cover.
The queen did not reveal who she was, thanked her and departed in the rain. The next day one of Her Majesty's servants returned the umbrella.
The old woman was beside herself for not giving her the best. She would have gladly given her the other one and missed an opportunity of a smile from the Queen.
How often do we give grudgingly and not do our best.
We think of our King as one who sits in Heaven on a throne, but He is also in the lowliest of us.

Ponder: Don't cry because it's over;
smile because it happened.

Today I am grateful for

Ponder Time

BE KIND

Be the light
☆☆☆☆☆☆

A Small Amount of Faith

When fog settles in we can't see very far ahead of us.
Driving is a nightmare as we drive slower and can't see
familiar landmarks. Schools delay opening until the fog lifts.
Our bathroom mirrors and windows "fog" over from the
steam. A wipe of a towel still does not rid
the moisture entirely.
Worry is like the fog which settles over us and clouds our
thoughts so we can't think clearly. We forget to trust God,
who can lift the moral fog of worry we are submerged in.
Lowell penned these words, "Beyond the dim unknown
standeth God, within the shadows,
keeping watch above his own."
We worry about the unknown. The Bible has examples
of people of faith who tried to solve problems on their own
to no avail. When they turned their worries over to God
he gave them the answers they needed.
Even a small amount of faith can accomplish much.
Luke 17:6
Faith is hoping in what is not seen. Hebrews 11:1

Ponder: Faith is the ability to not panic.

Today I am grateful for

Shine bright

Ponder Time

Be the light
✪✪✪✪✪

A Sign of Hope and Joy

The state of Kansas's nickname is the
Sunflower State and, of course, its state flower
is the sunflower.
The sunflower can grow as tall as 15 feet and always
toward the sun. They do look like a sun with their bright
yellow flowers extending from the center where the
seeds are formed.
The flowers appear to be a sign of hope and joy to many
who look at them. The sunflower has many uses such as
poultry feed, bird feed, oil, eaten as nuts, made into soap
and in the manufacturing of leather. No wonder they are
grown as a cash crop.
By comparison, the plants grow towards the light of the sun
and we grow in many ways in the light of God's son, Christ.
We can sow seeds of hope and give joy to those we
come in contact with.
Jesus said to the people, "I am the light of the world.
If you follow me you won't be stumbling through the
darkness, because you will have the light that leads to life."
John 8:12
He also said, "You are the light of the world—like a city on
a mountain, glowing in the light for all to see."
Matthew 5:14

Today I am grateful for

Ponder Time

Be the light

Called to be A Witness

In 1938 a Swedish nurse went to
Tanzania and set up a tent as a health post.
The local chief, Chongoma, refused to let his people
use her services. Later the chief's donkey developed a large
abscess on a leg. Chongoma brought this donkey to her to
do something but he made a comment to his people,
"If she claims to have powers to treat my people,
let her treat my donkey first."
With fear and trepidation, the nurse treated the donkey.
After a few days the donkey was healed. The chief
convened a public meeting to order his people to go to her
tent for all their health problems. People flocked to her tent.
Most were cured, and many more came.
This witness led many to Christianity.
The tent was replaced by a small mud hut. Later a
dispensary was built and it is now a major medical facility.
God works in mysterious ways.
Did he cause the donkey to have the abscess?
We are all called to be a witness for God
in whatever way we can.
"Christians are called to live holy lives among unbelievers."
John 17:14-19

Ponder: Happiness comes through doors you didn't even
know you left open.

Today I am grateful for

All THINGS are POSSIBLE

Ponder Time

_____
_____
_____
_____
_____
_____
_____
_____
_____
_____
_____

Be the light
☆☆☆☆☆☆

Wireless Messages

Wireless cell phones are very popular and
used by so many people because they are
convenient and portable. The media is full of ads
to buy their product at low rates.
One carrier in particular has the "can you hear me now?"
ad. They also state they are the most reliable network and
"we never stop working for you."
Cell phones also have a down side. If you should call 911
the call is sent to a dispatcher but they can't pinpoint your
exact location, which can cause delays.
Everything needs upgrades with new technology and this
will make an increase with a surcharge. This new technology
takes time and could take up to two years to upgrade the
entire state.
God has had wireless messages since the world began.
It is called prayer. He knows your exact location
and can give an instant response. He also claims he never
stops working for you, and is the most reliable.
Our part is to call him often
and let him know you are hearing him.
"Be anxious for nothing, but in everything by prayer and
supplication, with thanksgiving, let your requests be made
known to God." Philippians 4:6

Ponder: "It's like driving a car at night. You never see further
than your headlights, but you can make the
whole trip that way." E.L. Doctorow

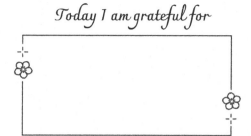

Today I am grateful for

Choose Peace

Ponder Time

Be the light

Measuring Up

Three of the gospel writers give us this same
message: "If you give, you will receive. Your gift will
return to you in full measure, pressed down, shaken
together to make room for more, and running over.
Whatever measure you use in giving–large or small, it will
be used to measure what is given back to you." Luke 6:38
We have been given the ten commandments and the
Beatitudes as guidelines to live by but sometimes our selfish
gain gets in the way of right living.
The Bible also tells us, "Don't forget to do good and to share
what you have with those in need, for such sacrifices
are very pleasing to God." Hebrews 13:16
Thankfulness brings praise to God.
"If you are ordered to court and your shirt is taken from you,
give your coat, too. If a soldier demands that you carry his
gear for a mile, carry it two miles." Matthew 5:40
Why should we withhold when we know how much the
Lord wants to bless us with all good things?
How do you measure up?

"Happiness is not so much in having, as sharing.
We make a living by what we get,
but we make a life by what we give." Norman MacEwan
Ponder: Plenty of people are willing to give God *credit*,
yet few are willing to give Him *cash*.

Today I am grateful for

you are
AMAZING

Ponder Time

Be the light
✿✿✿✿✿

Life's in the Details

It is human nature to fear the unknown. We worry about our health, our jobs, our security, our family, etc. What will be the results of the doctor's tests? Will I be able to keep my job or get another? Will I have enough to retire on?

Put yourself in Mary and Joseph's shoes. She was a teenager and he was a little older. They were due to have a baby and were traveling a long distance for a census in Bethlehem. Where would they stay with a large crowd expected to register and a limited budget? No one of her family could give her assurance or help. After Jesus' birth they were directed to flee to Egypt. Now where would they stay to keep a new baby warm and not exposed to the weather.

The Lord did provide a stable for Jesus' birth and caves along the way when traveling. The Wise Men, who brought gold, would help get them established for the two years in Egypt.

Most people, after their baby is born, want people to see their new one. But if Mary was homesick she couldn't go back home because of King Herold's threat. The Lord was watching over all the details of their lives. He does ours too, if we put our trust in Him and not fear the unknown.

For the Lord your God is living among you...
He will take delight in you with gladness.
With His love, He will calm all your fears.
He will rejoice over you with joyful songs. Zephaniah 3:17

Today I am grateful for

THE LORD IS MY
Light
AND
Salvation

PSALM 27:1

Ponder Time

Be the light
✦✦✦✦✦

Renewed Every Morning

The holiday rush is winding down and most people are experiencing a slump and a need to be rejuvenated.

The Lord is in the renewal business. He is always creating, building and reviving. He can restore us physically, spiritually or emotionally if we call on him.

Matthew 11:28 – Jesus said, "Come to me, all of you who are weary and carry heavy burdens, and I will give you rest. Take my yoke upon you. Let me teach you, because I am humble and gentle, and you will find rest for your souls."

The Psalmist gave many instances. A familiar one is in Psalms 103:5 – "Bless the Lord, who satisfies your mouth with good things, so that you will be renewed like the eagles."

For our health, "therefore we do not lose heart. Even though our outward man is perishing, yet the inward man is being renewed day by day." Jeremiah 30:17

"So, Rejoice in the Lord, O you righteous," Psalms 33:1

"God's faithfulness is great, being renewed every morning and his compassion never fails. My soul claims the Lord as my inheritance, therefore I will hope in him. The Lord is wonderfully good to those who wait for him, to those who seek for him." Lamentations 3:22-24

Ponder: "In order to have a real relationship with our creativity, we must take the time and care to cultivate it."
Julia Cameron

Today I am grateful for

Ponder Time

Be the light
☆☆☆☆☆☆☆

A Love that Doesn't Age

Love hath no season, Love hath no boundaries, Love hath no age, Love hath no race, Love hath no time limit and Love hath no social distinction. That's because God is Love and he is everywhere and does not discriminate. God loves us so much that he was willing to send his son to die on the cross for our sins.

"Greater love hath no man than this, that a man lay down his life for his friends." John 15:13

There seems to be more loving and out giving during the month of December and more so after the earthquake flood that caused so many lives to be lost in the Asian Gulf. One can't imagine the magnitude of the destruction and disaster that follows.

This has been a good time for the world to help supply and comfort those that are caught in unfortunate circumstances, and the need continues.

"Let us practice loving each other for love comes from God." 1 John 4:7

True joy comes when we share love with those less fortunate than ourselves. It is in giving that we receive.

For the Lord is good and His love endures forever; His faithfulness continues through all generations. Psalm 100:5

Today I am grateful for

Become the Change

Ponder Time

_____
_____
_____
_____
_____
_____
_____
_____
_____
_____
_____
_____

Be the light

What Is Your Passion

Most of us have a passion for something. It can cover a wide range of subjects. Passion means putting your heart and soul into something you love. It might be to be with your family, to achieve a goal, passion for animals, for privacy, your country, gardening, writing, music, sewing, painting, understanding, helping others, the environment, etc.
Whatever it is you spend a lot of your time and money doing it because you rank it high on your priorities.
For many years Passion Plays have been acted out live and reveal the love and sacrifice Christ made on our behalf. Then last year the movie, "The Passion of the Christ," was shown. Hollywood filmmakers did not want to attempt it, but Mel Gibson followed his heart and it was a bestseller coming out in time for Easter.
The world needs to hear this good news and change their thoughts to their creator who had his Son willingly die on the cross for our sins. This is what true passion is and it is the same for everyone who believes.

John 3:16 "For God so loved the world, that He gave His only begotten Son that whosoever believeth in Him should not perish but have everlasting life."

Ponder: Love is a work of art that two hearts create.

Today I am grateful for

Let's make TODAY beautiful

Ponder Time

Be the light

The Speck and I

Years ago a lady in Berlin told about
her neighbor across the street whose window
panes always looked so dingy. The lady seemed
to have an air of superiority and wondered why her
neighbor seemed content but with a little soap and water
they could let the light in.
Then the lady's stout cleaning maid came armed with a
bucket of cleaning supplies to do her windows. The lady left
for an hour or so while the maid did the work.
When she returned the windows sparkled and she looked
across the street and exclaimed, "Did my neighbors clean
their windows, too, while I was gone? They really shine!"
The maid answered without hesitation, "No, Maam, it was
your windows that were dirty."
The lady learned a lesson that can be found in
Luke 6: 41-42 "And why quibble about the speck in someone
else's eye—his little fault, when a board is in your own? How
can you think of saying to him, Brother, let me help you with a
speck in your eye, when you can't see past the board in
yours? Hypocrite! First get rid of the board, and then perhaps
you can see well enough to deal with the speck!"

Ponder: Retentive memory may be a good thing, but the
ability to forget is the mark of true greatness.

Today I am grateful for

Believe in Yourself

Ponder This

Be the light

On the Job Training

An apprentice is a person who works with an experienced person on the job training.
We all are novices when we are growing up and depend on parents, family, church, schools, etc. to learn new things and discipline.
Now many are going to school and getting credits for experience on the job.
The disciples were apprentices as they worked with Jesus and followed his teachings for the three years he was with them.
They were no different than we are and need instructions in rightful living. The Bible, church, family and friends can keep us in line. The Holy Spirit lets our conscience know when we are off course or are doing good. We are never too young or too old to be taught lessons in life.
Psalms 71:17 "O God, you have helped me from my earliest childhood-and I have constantly testified to others of the wonderful things you do. And now that I am old and gray, don't forsake me. Give me time to tell this new generation (and their children too) about all your mighty miracles."

"For the Lord grants wisdom! His every word is a treasure of knowledge and understanding."
Proverbs 2:6

Ponder: I've learned that a father's blessings can fill a son's soul to the brim. Kelley Tobey

Today I am grateful for

BE KIND

Ponder Time

Be the light

Knowing and Doing

A man went to apply for a job and as he was interviewed the employer said, "Let's go out for lunch and get better acquainted."
When the food was served the man started to salt his food without tasting it first.
The employer said nothing but later did not hire the applicant because he felt he would make hasty decisions without first getting all the facts.
Now is the time when more people are looking for summer jobs. Small details in speech, mannerisms, dress or attitude may be the reason they are not hired.
Common sense and your conscience are both gifts from God. If we would pay attention to them we would find ourselves in less trouble.
Proverbs 3:21 Have two goals; wisdom, that is knowing and doing right–and common sense.
Proverbs 14:33 Wisdom is enshrined in the hearts of men of common sense, but it must shout loudly before fools hear it.
"...The Lord your God will bless you in all your work and in everything you put your hand to."
Deuteronomy 15:10
Everything you do for the Lord matters, and everything you do for others is an expression of His abundant love.

Ponder: The straight and narrow path would not be so narrow if more people walked it.

Today I am grateful for

Shine bright

Ponder Time

_____
_____
_____
_____
_____
_____
_____
_____
_____
_____
_____

Be the light

You Have A Partner

During the Miss Universe Pageant, one of the finalists was asked, "What was your greatest failure and what did you learn from it?" Her immediate response was, "I didn't win in an earlier contest, but I learned from the experience and entered again."

Most of us hate to admit failures and would have to think about which was our worst one. We would be embarrassed to let the whole world know about it.

History is full of mistakes starting with Adam and Eve. Even Abraham Lincoln was defeated several times before he became President and look at his record.

We wish we could take back words, never been careless in driving, lost our patience or temper and did hurtful things. Getting even or revenge hurts the person doing it usually more than the other one involved.

Dwelling on past failures leaves us in a rut that is hard to get out of. Whining or complaining won't solve our problems unless we turn them over to the Lord and trust him for the solution.

1st Peter 4: 12-13 Dear Friends, Don't be bewildered or surprised when you go through the fiery trials ahead for this is no strange, unusual thing that is going to happen to you. Instead, be really glad—because these trials will make you partners with Christ in his suffering, and afterwards you will have the wonderful joy of sharing his glory in that coming day when it will be displayed.

Ponder: Real friends are those who, when you've made a fool of yourself, don't feel that you've done a permanent job.

Today I am grateful for

TRUST THE TIMING OF YOUR LIFE

Ponder Time

Be the light

 # Do You Have A Filter

This is the age when we filter so many everyday
things such as coffee filters, air, water, gas filters and we
can screen our computers, internet, films, etc.
While most are to our advantage some can be more harmful
to our mind, eyes, heart, emotions and to others. The media
blows it up because of the prices paid for by the sponsors.
Many films and music are disgraceful.
Now we are seeing the results of bullying, action games
and films that are so real and instructions on
how to commit crimes.
The Bible is clear that we can filter out much of the trash we
are exposed to. God says you are wonderfully made and
knows your thoughts before you say them. We can choose to
shut off the computer, not listen to degrading music, foul
language or not attend films that are "X" rated.
Psalms 37:4-6 "Be delighted with the Lord. Then he will
give you all your heart's desires. Commit everything you do
to the Lord. Trust him to help you do it and he will.
Your innocence will be clear to everyone."

Ponder: We cannot expect other people to see eye to eye
with us if we look down on them.

Today I am grateful for

All THINGS are POSSIBLE

Ponder Time

Be the light

My Record Book

More and more we hear about a new scheme to rip off an innocent victim. One of the latest is identity theft and the person taken advantage of doesn't know about it until a good deal of money has been taken from their accounts. The hard part is to then trace it to the thief. It can take months of anguish to try to and settle the fraud.

Sometimes there is more than one person by the same name, especially in families named after a parent or grandparent, which makes it harder to clarify their identity. D.N.A., fingerprints, Social Security numbers help but these are not foolproof.

So how does God keep track of everyone in such a complex world?

Psalms 139:13-16 has his answer. "You made all the delicate inner parts of my body, and knit them together in my mothers's womb. Thank you for making me so wonderfully complex! It is amazing to think about. Your workmanship is marvelous—and how well I know it. You were there while I was being formed in utter seclusion! You saw me before I was born and scheduled each day of my life before I began to breathe. Every day was recorded in your Book!"

Isn't this nice that the Lord has no problem keeping track of his children? When judgment day comes he won't get you mixed up with another person by the same name. We will still have earthly identity problems but our heavenly identity will be assured.

Ponder: By the time a person gets to greener pastures, they can't climb the fence.

Today I am grateful for

Choose Peace

Ponder Time

128

Be the light

An Added Bonus

Everyone likes a bonus. Maybe it's an end of the year gift, a paid vacation or something extra thrown in a purchase. It might be a reward or something more you weren't counting on.

This fall season is a bonus to farmers with the hot weather to dry up the crops for harvesting. Some are reporting high yields. The warm weather is a bonus on utilities. Answered prayer for healing or an expense was less than expected or a purchase that was a bargain are all bonuses. We often say it's good luck but God has a hand in all events of our lives. The timing of things beyond our control is a miracle and we marvel at the coincidence.

All the bonuses in our daily lives are blessings from God, such as our health, ability to work, our homes, food to eat, family and friends. Hope, peace, courage, mercy, patience, guidance, etc. are things that cannot be bought or sold. Christians have an added bonus for a hope for eternity in Heaven.

We should thank God daily for all these added bonuses in our lives. When we see the victims' homes, completely wiped out in the hurricanes, wars or famine, we should praise God and be thankful He has provided our cup to overflow.

Ponder: Inflation hasn't ruined everything.
A dime can still be used as a screwdriver.

Today I am grateful for

you are
AMAZING

Ponder Time

Be the light
✿✿✿✿✿✿✿

How Wise Were
the Wise Men

Mary, Joseph and baby Jesus didn't stay long in the stable. Travelers to Jerusalem returned home and they were able to stay in a house.
Previously the astrologers from the East had been tracking this star for two years. When they got to Jerusalem to inquire of King Herod, "Where is the newborn King of the Jews? For we have seen his star in far-off eastern lands, and have come to worship him."
Naturally, King Herod was deeply disturbed. He didn't want anyone to usurp his reign. King Herod called a meeting of the religious leaders and they confirmed the prophecy was Bethlehem.
Sure enough the star appeared to these wise men and stopped at the house where the baby and his mother were. They gave him gifts of gold, frankincense and myrrh. They were wiser still when the Lord appeared to them in a dream to return home another way.
When King Herod found out they had disobeyed him he ordered all baby boys 2 years and under to be killed. How cruel to take the lives of innocent babies for his revenge. So Joseph, Mary and Jesus fled to Egypt to escape his wrath.
The wise men were wise in astrology, traveling on camels long distance in search of the newborn King and wiser still to not report to King Herod.
We can be much wiser, too, if we listen to God.
Ponder: An unusual child is one who asks questions that his parents can answer.

Today I am grateful for

THE LORD IS MY
Light
AND
Salvation
PSALM 27:1

Ponder Time

Be the light

A Few New Beatitudes

Blessed are those who can laugh at themselves: they will always find something to laugh at.

Blessed are they who can tell the difference between a mountain and a molehill:
they will be spared a lot of trouble.

Blessed are those who can rest and sleep without looking for excuses: they will become wise.

Blessed are those who know how to keep still and listen; they will learn something new.

Blessed are those who are smart enough not to take themselves seriously; they will be appreciated by their fellow man.

Happy are you if you can look at little things seriously and at serious things peacefully; you will go far.

Happy are you if you can always give a kindly interpretation to others' attitudes, even in the face of appearance to the contrary; people will think you are a bit stupid, but this is the price of charity.

Happy are you if you can appreciate a smile and forget a frown; your path will be sunny.

Blessed are those who think before they act and who pray before they think; they will avoid plenty of mistakes.

Happy are you if you can hold your tongue and smile when you are interrupted, contradicted, or put down; the gospel is beginning to penetrate your heart.

Happy are you and truly blessed if you can recognize the Lord in everyone you meet; you have found the true light, you have found real wisdom.

DEAR GOD,
SO FAR TODAY, GOD, I'VE DONE ALL RIGHT.
I HAVEN'T GOSSIPED, HAVEN'T LOST MY
TEMPER, HAVEN'T BEEN GREEDY, GRUMPY,
NASTY, SELFISH, OR OVER-INDULGENT. I'M
REALLY GLAD ABOUT THAT.
BUT, IN A FEW MINUTES, GOD, I'M GOING
TO GET OUT OF BED, AND FROM THEN ON
I'M PROBABLY GOING TO NEED A LOT MORE
HELP. - John Michael Talbot

I AM A CHRISTIAN

When I say, "I am a Christian,"
I'm not shouting, "I'm clean livin'."
I'm whispering, "I was lost,
Now I'm found and forgiven."

When I say, "I am a Christian,"
I don't speak of this with pride.
I'm confessing that I stumble
And need Christ to be my guide.

When I say, "I am a Christian,"
I'm not trying to be strong,
I'm professing that I'm weak
And need His strength to carry on.

When I say, "I am a Christian,"
I'm not bragging of success.
I'm admitting I have failed
And need God to clean my mess.

When I say, "I am a Christian,"
I still feel the sting of pain.
I have my share of heartaches
So I call upon His name.

When I say, "I am a Christian,"
I'm not holier than thou,
I'm just a simple sinner
Who received God's grace somehow!
Author Unknown

Subject: Ark

Everything I need to know, I learned from Noah's Ark...
1. Don't miss the boat.
2. Remember that we are all in the same boat.
3. Plan ahead. It wasn't raining when Noah built the Ark.
4. Stay fit. When you're 600 years old, someone may ask you to do something really big.
5. Don't listen to critics; just get on with the job that needs to be done.
6. Build your future on high ground.
7. For safety's sake, travel in pairs.
8. Speed isn't always an advantage. The snails were on board with the cheetahs.
9. When you're stressed, float for a while.
10. Remember, the Ark was built by amateurs; the Titanic professionals.
11. No matter the storm, when you are with God, there's always a rainbow waiting.   God Bless

HOW DO YOU SPEND YOUR DASH?

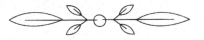

I read of a man who stood to speak,
At the funeral of a friend.
He referred to the dates on his tombstone,
From the beginning - to the end.

He noted that first came the date of his birth,
Then he spoke his death date with tears.
But he said what mattered most of all,
Was the dash between those years.

For that dash represents all the time,
That he spent alive on earth -
And now only those who loved him,
Know what that little dash is worth.

For it matters not how much we own,
The cars - the house - the cash.
What matters is how we lived and loved,
And how we spent our dash.

So when your eulogy's being read,
With your life's actions to rehash,
Would you be proud of the things they say
About how you spent your dash?

Linda Ellis

THINGS I'VE LEARNED

I've learned—
that you can do something in an instant
that will give you heartache for life.

I've learned—
that either you control your attitude or
it controls you.

I've learned—
that sometimes when I'm angry I have the
right to be angry, but that doesn't give me
the right to be cruel.

IT'S IN THE VALLEYS I GROW

Sometimes life seems hard to bear,
>> Full of sorrow, trouble and woe
>> It's then I have to remember
>> That it's in the valleys I grow.

If I always stayed on the mountain top
>> And never experienced pain,
>> I would never appreciate God's love
>> And would be living in vain.

I have so much to learn
>> And my growth is very slow,
>> Sometimes I need the mountain tops,
>> But it's in the valleys I grow.

I do not always understand
>> Why things happen as they do,
>> But I am very sure of one thing
>> My Lord will see me through.

My little valleys are nothing
>> When I picture Christ on the cross
>> He went through the valley of death;
>> His victory was Satan's loss.

Forgive me Lord, for complaining
>> When I'm feeling so very low.
>> Just give a gentle reminder
>> That it's in the valleys I grow.

Continue to strengthen me, Lord
>> And use my life each day
>> To share your love with others
>> And help them find their way.

Thank you for valleys, Lord
>> For this one thing I know
>> The mountain tops are glorious
>> But it's in the valleys I grow!

JESUS PRAYS FOR YOU

Close your eyes and imagine Jesus on His knees praying
for you.
His lips, and it is your name he speaks. He talks about your tasks,
relationships, and needs. He knows who you are. Jesus prays that
your sickness will be healed, your hurt assuaged, and your
brokenness mended.
As he prays for you, Jesus commends your desire and compliments
your efforts. He applauds your accomplishments and achievements.
He speaks for your dreams and asks that you have the courage to
pursue them. Jesus sets his heart on what is best for you and prays
that you be immensely blessed.
The Bible says praying for you is so important to Jesus that he lives
in order to do so.
Nothing strengthens me more, dear God, than to perceive that
Jesus is on his knees praying for me. Amen

BE SAFE

1.　Avoid riding in automobiles because they are responsible for 20% of all fatal accidents.
2.　Do not stay home because 17% of all accidents occur in the home.
3.　Avoid walking the streets or sidewalks because 17% of all accidents occur to pedestrians.
4.　Avoid traveling by air, rail, or water because 16% of all accidents involve these forms of transportation.
5.　Of the remaining 33%, 32% of all deaths occur in hospitals. Above all else, avoid hospitals.

You will be pleased to learn that only .001% of all deaths occur in worship services in church, and these are usually related to previous physical disorders. Therefore, logic tells us that the safest place for you to be at any given point in time is at church!

Bible study is safe, too. The percentage of deaths during Bible study is even less.

FOR SAFETY'S SAKE - ATTEND CHURCH AND READ YOUR BIBLE... IT COULD SAVE YOUR LIFE!

A father was approached by his small son,
who told him proudly,
"I know what the Bible means!"
His father smiled and replied, "What do you
mean, you 'know' what the Bible means?"
The son replied, "I do know!"
"Okay," said his father.
"So, Son, what does the Bible mean?"
"That's easy, Daddy. It stands for,

" Basic Information Before Leaving Earth."

HYMN SING-A-LONG
We have a hymn for everyone

The Dentist's Hymn
Crown Him with Many Crowns

The Realtor's Hymn
I've Got a Mansion, Just Over the Hilltop

The Weatherman's Hymn
There Shall Be Showers of Blessings

The Massage Therapists Hymn
He Touched Me

The Contractor's Hymn
The Church's One Foundation

The Doctor's Hymn
The Great Physician

The Tailor's Hymn
Holy, Holy, Holy

AND FOR YOU MOTORISTS

The Golfer's Hymn
There is a Green Hill Far Away

45 mph
God Will Take Care of You

The Politician's Hymn
Standing On The Promises

55 mph
Guide Me, O Thou Great Jehovah

The Optometrist's Hymn
Open My Eyes that I Might See

65 mph
Nearer My God To Thee

The IRA Agent's Hymn
I Surrender All

75 mph
Nearer Still Nearer

The Gossip's Hymn
Pass It On

85 mph
This World Is Not My Home

The Electrician's Hymn
Send the Light

95 mph
Lord, I'm Coming Home

The Shopper's Hymn
Sweet By and By

Over 100 mph
Precious Memories

SLOW ME DOWN

Slow me down, Lord, I'm going too fast;
I can't see my brother when he's walking past.
I miss a lot of good things day by day.
I don't know a blessing when it comes my way.
Slow me down, Lord, I want to see
more of the things that are good for me.
A little less of me and a little more of You.
I want the heavenly atmosphere to trickle through.
Let me help a brother when the going is rough;
When folks work together, life isn't so tough.
Slow me down, Lord, so I can talk
With some of your angels as they walk.
Author unknown

The Master's Touch

Wishing to encourage her young son's progress at the piano, a mother took her son to a Paderewski concert. After being seated, the mother spotted a friend in the audience and walked over to greet her. Seizing the opportunity to explore the concert hall, the little boy rose and explored his way through a door marked, "NO ADMITTANCE." When the lights dimmed and the concert was about to begin, the mother returned to her seat to find her son missing. Suddenly the curtains parted and the spotlight focused on the Steinway on stage. To her horror the mother saw her little boy sitting at the keyboard picking out "Twinkle, Twinkle, Little Star."

At that moment the master made his entrance, moved to the piano, and whispered in the boy's ear, "Don't quit. Keep playing." He then leaned over, reached down with his left hand and began filling in a bass part. Soon his right arm reached around the other side of the child and he added a running obbligato. Together, the master, Paderewski, and the novice transformed the situation into a wonderfully creative experience. The audience was mesmerized.

That's the way it is with our Heavenly Father. What we can accomplish on our own is hardly noteworthy. We try our best but the results aren't exactly graceful, flowing music. But with the hand of the Master, our life's work truly can be beautiful.

Next time you set out to accomplish something, listen carefully. You can hear the Master's voice whispering in your ear, "Don't quit. Keep playing." Feel his loving arms around you. Know that his strong hands are there helping you turn your feeble attempt into true masterpieces. Remember, God doesn't call the equipped. He equips the called.

CHRISTMAS REMINDERS

May the Christmas *gifts* remind you of God's greatest gift,
His only begotten Son.
May the Christmas *candles* remind you of Him who is the
"Light of the World."
May the Christmas *trees* remind you of another tree upon which
He died for you.
May the Christmas *cheer* remind you of Him who said,
"Be of good cheer."
May the Christmas *bell* remind you of the glorious proclamation of
His birth.
May the Christmas *carols* remind you of the song the angels sang,
"Glory to God in the highest."
May the Christmas *season* remind you in every way of
Jesus Christ your king!

146

Imagine That

A High School religion teacher asked the
class to answer the question:
"What is a sin of omission?" One student
wrote, "A sin I should have committed but I didn't."
If you were to answer the question, what would you say?
It isn't one of the Ten Commandments but we do it very
often. Probably the biggest one is we forget.
We fail to heed a message and realize too late the
consequences. Maybe we forgot to write down a check,
missed a deadline, a birthday, a traffic no-no, etc.
We neglected to do something or had an oversight. The
newspapers leave out a person's name or give credit to the
one not deserving of it.
Perhaps you cheated on your income tax or deliberately
took advantage of someone.
Parents and teachers keep giving sage advice to the youth
who don't pay much attention until they get into trouble.
When they're older they wish they had listened or
applied themselves better.
The greatest of all faults is to imagine that we have none.
"Thy word have I hid in my heart
that I may not sin against thee." Psalm 119:11

Ponder: It is a good idea to keep your words soft and sweet,
you never know when you may have to eat them.
Andy Rooney

Today I am grateful for

Ponder Time

Be the light

Man Versus Cat

A priest in Brazil never liked cats. The neighborhood cats chose the roof of his rectory to do their nighttime games. He tried stones, a broom handle to the ceiling but all to no avail.
To irk him even more the cat next door would sit all day long on a wall that separated the houses. She would look at him with hatred in her eyes to defy him. This went on for a very long time with each ignoring the other.
Then one day the priest discovered he had rats in his house. He had no success with traps or bait. He sure could use that cat, but how could he entice her?
He put out a saucer of milk some distance from his kitchen door. The cat watched but did nothing for the two weeks he kept doing it. Then one day he saw the cat drinking the milk. Slowly she got used to it so everyday he placed the milk a little closer to the kitchen. After two more weeks the cat started living in his house and now the rats are gone.
We don't know who converted who, the man or the cat.
Do we have our mind set on people we don't like and keep our distance from them?
Matthew 5:43-45 "There is a saying, 'Love your friends and hate your enemies.' But I say: Love your enemies. Pray for those who persecute you. In that way you will be acting as true sons of your Father in heaven."

Ponder: Attitude is the mind's paintbrush-
it can color any situation.

Today I am grateful for

Become the Change

Ponder Time

Be the light

His Mighty Power

Jesus has many names. The ones we
hear most often are Christ, King of Kings,
Lord of Lords and Prince of Peace.
We also have earthly kingdoms. England has a royal family
that reigns but it also has a parliamentary government of a
House of Lords and a House of Commons. Some countries
have a Prince that rules and some even have
bad ones that are warlord.
These people can only rule during their lifetime, and be
overthrown or ousted. What power they have is limited
in most cases.
But Jesus' kingdom has no end and nothing can compare to
his mighty power. He is the only one who can restore peace
because he is the Prince of Peace. We crown him Lord of all
because he is the Almighty King.
Many of our hymns praise Him because He is our Savior
and sacrificed his life that we might spend eternity with Him.
Praise ye the Lord, Hallelujah!
"Let the peace of Christ rule in your hearts, since as
members of one body you were called to peace.
And be thankful." Colossians 3:15

Ponder: You can either remember and regret
or forget and have peace.

Today I am grateful for

Let your
light
Shine

Ponder Time

_____
_____
_____
_____
_____
_____
_____
_____
_____
_____
_____
_____
_____
_____
_____
_____
_____

Be the light

Slow Down and Wait

The Apostle Paul made three missionary
journeys and established many new churches
in Asia Minor. Later he was imprisoned in Rome
and wanted to keep track of the new churches lest they fall
back into their old habits. He also wanted to encourage
and comfort the new believers.
His messenger, Timothy, kept him posted and Paul wrote
letters to these churches and sent them back with Timothy.
Paul wrote many of these letters, which are now in the New
Testament, while he was in jail.
God has had them preserved and made available to us.
People today make the same sins as years ago and so they
are for our benefit also.
Did God allow Paul to be imprisoned so he had plenty of
time to have these letters recorded for our use?
Perhaps some setbacks we endure are times for us to slow
down and give God praise for what he is doing for us.

"But we must keep trusting God for something that hasn't
happened yet, it teaches us to wait patiently and confidently."
Romans 8:25

Ponder: Don't allow "hurry" to rule your lives.

Today I am grateful for

Ponder Time

Be the light

An Honest Mistake

A grandfather was telling his grandson a story
that happened to him years ago. The grandfather
had gone to the country store and made a purchase. After
he got home he realized a mistake had been made and
he owed the owner some more money.
The man could have waited until the next day but he made
the effort to return it that day.
That evening the store was robbed and the police were
called. They asked, "Who were the last people in the store?"
The owner said, "The grandfather and another man but he
could vouch for the grandfather's honesty."
We remember Abraham Lincoln for his honesty and he
was called, "Honest Abe." George Washington was also
known for not telling a lie.
If you tell the truth you don't need to tell lies to try and
cover up your wrong doing.
The 9th commandment is, "Thou shalt not lie."
Ephesians 4:25 "Stop lying to each other, tell the truth, for
we are all parts of each other and when we lie to each other
we are hurting ourselves.

Ponder: One reason why a dog is such a loveable creature
is that his tail wags instead of his tongue.

Today I am grateful for

Become
the
Change

Ponder Time

_____
_____
_____
_____
_____
_____
_____
_____
_____
_____
_____

Be the light

Tears of Joy
and Sorrow

Tears are a vital part of our lives and serve as an emotional release. Sometimes it can be in pain, grief, joy or just cleansing the eyes. These are a wide range of emotions.

The shortest verse in the Bible is, "Jesus wept." John 11:35 He was weeping over Lazarus' death. We know how sad Peter felt after denying Christ three times when he wept bitterly.

We can share in another's sorrow and cry with them but never say a word and it gives comfort and understanding.

You can be overwhelmed with joy and the tears flow in gratitude such as good news from a doctor, the birth of a child, a loved one returning, receiving an honor, etc.

We think of Christ dying on the cross for our sins and many people were weeping. Most of the disciples fled because they feared for their own lives.

Mary Magdalene went on Easter morning to the tomb. The angels asked her why she was crying. Then she recognized the risen Jesus and she was overjoyed. She was the one who had sat at Jesus' feet, washed his feet with her tears and dried them with her hair.

Praise the Lord for giving us tears.

Ponder: Life is continuously a mixed blessing.
It's up to YOU how you take it.

Today I am grateful for

Let's make today beautiful

Ponder Time

Be the light

Love Into Action

The writings by Mark in the New
Testament record Jesus as a servant of God.
We know he washed the disciples' feet at the Last Supper.
All the three years he spent ministering, people flocked to
hear him, wanted healing or being fed, etc. At times he
needed to go away by himself and spend time in
prayer with God.
We talk about giving up something for Lent and it is
easier said than done.
God would prefer we spend time as a servant helping others
in need. The recent major storm created electric outages and
the ice and snow left people stranded or in
need of shelter.
The utility workers and road crews and others put in many
extra hours. Neighbors and friends took time to watch and
check on one another.
Jesus' greatest commandment is: "You shall love the Lord
your God with all your heart, and with all your soul, and with
all your mind. This is the first and greatest commandment.
And the second is like it.
You shall love your neighbor as yourself." Matthew 22:38
This pleases the Lord to put our love into action.

Ponder: The secret of happy living is not to do what you like,
but to like what you do.

Today I am grateful for

Believe
in
Yourself

Ponder This

Be the light

Life Began
in a Garden

One song we often sing at Easter is,
"In the Garden." This is where Mary Magdalene met
Jesus, the divine Gardener, after his resurrection.
We also remember life started in a garden,
the Garden of Eden.
We think of a garden as a place to plant seeds and grow
fruits, vegetables, trees, flowers, etc.
It is a time of new beginnings.
Spring is a time of awakening the soil
after the sun warms it, and the rains refresh it.
Our lives are like the garden. If we have had setbacks we
can turn to the Divine Gardener to nurture us back. He can
plant the seeds of hope and love to help us grow into the
Christian faith he instills in us every day.
Many of the youth are graduating and will start new
beginnings. We can all be workers in God's garden and
make sure they stay on the right path with tender care.
Our Divine Gardener will always keep watch over them
too and see them blossom into the person
God plans for their future.

Ponder: Give time and love to your children
and you will be richly repaid.

Today I am grateful for

BE KIND

Ponder Time

Be the light

 What's That Aroma

People like to be outdoors now that the
weather is warmer. One of the things you
notice is the fragrance in the air from lilacs, peonies,
roses, fresh garden produce, flowering trees, etc.
God put all that fragrance into the air for us to enjoy.
But did you know you are a fragrance to God?
2 Corinthians 2:14-15, "But thanks be to God!
For through what Christ has done,
he has triumphed over us so that wherever we go
he uses us to tell others about the Lord and to spread
the Gospel like a sweet perfume. As far as God is
concerned, that is a sweet, wholesome fragrance in
our lives. It is the fragrance of Christ within us, an aroma
to both the saved and unsaved all around us."
It pleases God that we are a life giving perfume to others
when we know Christ and spread his word in action or
praise. Isn't that nice to be called a sweet fragrance?
Better yet we can do it all year long.

Ponder: A youngster's idea of a balanced meal is
a cookie in both hands.

Today I am grateful for

Shine bright

Ponder Time

_____
_____
_____
_____
_____
_____
_____
_____
_____
_____
_____
_____

Be the light

Age Is A Process

Winthrop, Iowa, just celebrated its 150 years
with many people returning who grew up here.
The town is not the same as they remembered it.
Many landmarks are gone and replaced with new things.
The people have changed as well as the visitors.
Age is a process we can't control.
When Jesus began his ministry, at age 30, the people
noticed a big change. He was no longer the son of Joseph
or a carpenter as they knew him. They flocked to him now
because he could heal, preach and supply their needs.
When we become a Christian we change, too. We are like
babies that require milk. The more we mature in Christ and
follow his teachings then we are able to take on solid food.
We show kindness, love, patience, and service, etc.
Hebrews 5:12,13 - You are like babes who can only drink
milk, not old enough for solid food. And when a person is still
living on milk it shows he isn't very far along in the Christian
life, and doesn't know much about the difference between
right and wrong. He is still a baby Christian!
You will never be able to eat solid spiritual food and
understand the deeper things of God's word until you
become a better Christian and learn right from wrong by
practicing doing right.
Proverbs 4:11 A life of doing right is the wisest life there is.

Ponder: In the cookie of life, friends are the chocolate chips.

Today I am grateful for

TRUST THE TIMING OF YOUR LIFE

Ponder Time

Be the light

Throw Away Society

We have become a throw away
society and are ruining God's pristine
beaches, rivers, soil and air. Every summer
people clean up tons of garbage that others have
tossed in the rivers and on the beaches.
It looks great after the cleanup but the next year they
can do it all over again.
Plastic bags kill dolphins who think they are food, pop tabs
are shiny and attract sea birds, chemicals kill fish and the
rivers are filled with silt and run offs that prohibit swimming.
When God created the world he said it was good.
There was a balance that allowed food for survival.
People are mining and cutting down trees and that
disrupts nature.
Why should a few careless people spoil God's handiwork?
We are making an effort to clean up the roadsides and
water. Air pollution is one of the worst. If each of us made a
concerted effort to protect the planet it would help us all and
future generations.
God does not dump us when we make mistakes.
He rescues us and cleans us up after we are sorry for the
mess we make in our lives.

Ponder: If the house is messy and company drops by, get
the vacuum sweeper out and say you're starting to clean!

Today I am grateful for

Ponder Time

_____
_____
_____
_____
_____
_____
_____
_____
_____
_____

All THINGS are POSSIBLE

Be the light

Shine and Glow

We go to great lengths to polish a lot of things;
our furniture, cars, pots and pans, shoes, our teeth, etc.
We take pride in making them shine and glow,
which might appear selfish.
Do we put as much effort into our discipleship of keeping
ourselves polished and aglow, in plain view for everyone to
see? Attending church on Sunday is one way but there are
six more days in the week. Taking time to pray, read Scripture
and putting forth the effort to do for others is what Jesus
wants us to polish up on and shine for him.
Remember the song, "This Little Light of Mine,
I'm Going To Let It Shine?"
This makes you happy, others happy and Jesus happy.
This also requires action. We are connected to God, the
source of all power. When we apply ourselves to do
his will we replenish the light within us
so we can share the light and
reflect God's light.

Ponder: A smile is a curve that can set a lot of things straight.

Today I am grateful for

Choose Peace

Ponder Time

Be the light

Almost Nothing

About five years ago a man in West Virginia
won the nearly 315 million Powerball game. He
opted for the lump payment of 170 million -
93 million after taxes.
He was already a self made millionaire but this has
drastically changed his life. His wife left him and his
drug addicted granddaughter, his protege and heir, died when
17 year old. He has struggled with drinking, gambling and
philandering and the media loves to tell of his transgressions.
He has no friends because everyone wants to borrow
money or something. Once they borrow from you,
you can't be friends anymore, he says.
He and his wife used to go to church but now everyone
has a sob story.
He has built two churches, gives to charities, scholarships,
etc., but life isn't the same. Money isn't everything.
We hear this all the time with young celebrity singers,
sports players or movie stars.
The Apostle Paul said in Philippians 4:12,13 - I know how
to live on almost nothing or with everything. I have learned
the secret of contentment in every situation, whether it is a
full stomach or hunger, plenty or want. For I can do
everything God asks me to do with the help of Christ who
gives me the strength and power.

Hebrews 13:5 Stay away from the love of money,
be satisfied with what you have.
For God has said, "I will never, never fail you
nor forsake you."

Ponder: A pat on the back is only a few vertebrates away
from a kick in the behind, but it does a great deal more.

Today I am grateful for

you are
AMAZING

Ponder Time

Be the light

cA Humble Servant

Jesus could have been born in a castle or
mansion but instead God chose to have everyday
common parents and a humble stable for his birth.
If Christ had been born in a castle the lower class of people
couldn't relate to him at all.
His whole life was spent as a humble servant. He didn't
have a home and everyone wanted something from him.\
The disciples he chose were not the educated priests but
lower class fishermen. On the cross he humbled himself
and was placed in a tomb that wasn't his own.
What a contrast between the rich and the famous. He has
continued to be honored all these years and others well
known are forgotten.
In more recent years we see a big contrast between Queen
Elizabeth of England and Princess Diana. Queen Elizabeth
seems aloof in public and always wears gloves. Princess Di
was involved with humanity and 10 years now after her
death she is still remembered as the People's Princess.

Ponder: Footprints in the sands of time
are never made by sitting down.

Today I am grateful for

THE LORD IS MY
Light
AND
Salvation

PSALM 27:1

Ponder Time

174

Be the light

One Fixed Point

If you look at old photo albums you notice right away the hair styles, clothes, cars, etc. They can really date the years they were in style.

Now we have new technology on about everything and even from year to year the things are outdated and are replaced by a new item. Even our records need to be updated.

All things either wear out or go out of style. Our bodies are also in a gradual change.

But not God. He's the only thing that does not change. Imagine all the thousands of years that have passed and he doesn't grow old.

Jesus called himself "Alpha and Omega, the beginning and the end." God is the hub around which the Universe revolves. The only way to understand a changing world is to relate it to its one fixed point—God.

Hebrews 13-8 "Jesus Christ is the same yesterday, today and forever." This is the one promise to each generation that he is always with us and has plans for eternity if we believe. Give praise to the Lord.

We love because He first loved us. 1 John 4:19

Today I am grateful for

Ponder Time

Be the light
✩✩✩✩✩✩✩✩✩✩✩

Polish Your Qualities

A ten year old boy sat polishing his trumpet
a few minutes before the morning worship started.
"What a nice shine on that horn!" the group's
director commented.
"Thank you," the boy replied. "My grandfather's here this
morning and he's deaf. I thought if I put on a real good shine
he could at least enjoy the glow."
He could at least enjoy the glow...this child had the right
qualities in him to show he cared for others and wanted his
message to glow.
Love is caring for others and it brings joy to them and it
pleases you as well. There are lots of people who need a
smile, a helping hand, time to just listen or pray for them.
We need to polish our communications style so that we
can reach more people and share God's love.

If we love one another, God dwelleth in us, and his love
is perfected in us. 1 John 4:12

Ponder: Children are likely to live up to what you
believe of them. Lady Bird Johnson

Today I am grateful for

Become the Change

Ponder Time

_____
_____
_____
_____
_____
_____
_____
_____
_____
_____
_____

178

Be the light

Who Cared

The entire Jewish council brought Jesus
before Pilate, the governor. They began
accusing him of leading the people to ruin by
telling them not to pay their taxes to the Roman
government and claiming he was their
Messiah—a King.
Pilate turned to the chief priests and to the mob
and said, "This isn't a crime."
Then he was taken to King Herod. His soldiers mocked him
and ridiculed him and sent him back to Pilate because he did
nothing to call for the death penalty. He was scourged with
leather thongs and released.
A prisoner could be freed but the mob became more violent
and demanded Jesus to be crucified instead of Barabbas.
Three times Pilate demanded,
"What crime has he committed?"
The mob got louder and louder until Pilate gave in for them
to do as they wished. So Jesus was taken away to be
crucified.
How easily a mob can get out of control by a few inciting it.
Worse yet was Pilate's weakness by being influenced by a
mob. There should have been a trial and jury but no one took
charge. Since it was time for the Passover they wanted to get
it over with hastily. Who cared if Jesus was innocent?
It was probably all of God's plan to have Jesus sentenced to
death. He paid the supreme sacrifice for our sins so we might
have salvation. Praise Jesus for the suffering on the cross
for our sins.
Jesus said, "I came that they may have life, and have it
abundantly." John 10:7, 10:10b

Today I am grateful for

Let's make today beautiful

Ponder Time

Be the light

Testing of Your Faith

The Apostle Paul complained about a thorn
in his side. He had many other pains in his
life—imprisoned with shackles, mistreated, etc.
No one goes through life without some thorns to
contend with. They may be disappointments, failure,
loneliness, poor health, divorce, grief, etc.
We want to complain, "Why me?"
Then we think what Jesus had to suffer. He was rejected
by many, abandoned by his disciples but the worst was his
dying on the cross for our sins. He was whipped with pieces
of sharp bones that cut into his back, a crown of thorns was
wedged onto his head and humiliated to carry his own cross
to Calvary. There he was nailed to the cross for 6 hours
and endured the taunts and agonizing pain.
So how far did Jesus have to carry his own cross?
The traditional path from Pilate's praetorium through the
Old City of Jerusalem to the church of the Holy Sepulchre,
as it exists today, is 650 yards long, which is a little over a
third of a mile. Simon of Cyrene was forced to help him
carry the cross.
When we complain, read James 1:2-4 which says,
"Consider it pure joy, my brothers, we know that the testing
of your faith brings perseverance. Perseverance must
finish its work so that you may be mature and complete,
not lacking in anything.

Ponder: Old age is defined as when broad minds and
narrow waists start changing places.

Today I am grateful for

Believe
in
Yourself

Ponder This

Be the light

Our Foundation

Jesus had 12 disciples but the Bible says he had a chosen few who were with him on special occasions. At his transfiguration Peter, James and John were the only ones on the mountain top to witness this.

At the Garden of Gethsemane Jesus shared deep anguish with his closest friends, Peter, James and John. His human anxiety showed and he gave them an opportunity to minister to him in his time of need even though he was under his Father's care.

Mary Magdalene and Mary, the mother of James and Joseph, watch from a distance at his crucifixion. The women were first at the tomb on Easter morning.

Joseph of Arimathea, of the Jewish Supreme Court, asked for his body and prepared it for burial and placed it in a tomb. John was present at his crucifixion because Jesus turned to his mother and told John to look after her.

We also need close friends and family to share our innermost thoughts and concerns and a larger circle of friends we can also depend upon.

The foundation of our church is, "Faith, Family, Friends, and Fun." We truly need the support of all of these to strengthen our faith and witness to others by prayer and service.

Jesus said "You are my friends." Luke 12:4 and we can count on him to befriend us.

We have shared together the blessings of God.

Philippians 1:7

Today I am grateful for

Ponder Time

BE KIND

Be the light

Life's Interruptions

Our lives are full of interruptions every day.
Some are good and some are bad–phone calls,
lost articles, families with small children, illness
and even bad weather.
Jesus' ministry was full of interruptions. He restored a blind
man's sight, a paralyzed man was able to walk, a woman's
son brought back to life, even sending word to heal a sick
girl, feeding the multitudes, etc. Everywhere he went he was
stopped to supply a need.
Once, some mothers brought their little children to Jesus to
have them blessed. The disciples shooed them away, telling
them not to bother him. But when Jesus saw what was
happening he was very much displeased and said to them,
"Let the children come to me, for the kingdom of God belongs
to such as they. Don't send them away." Then he took the
children into his arms and placed his hands on their heads
and blessed them. Mark 10:13-14
Maybe the interruption in your day may be a prayer for
someone needing it. You could be an angel of mercy, a
helping hand, a listening ear or giving advice. An act of
kindness is very important no matter how simple.
If Jesus could take time out of his busy days for others,
so then can we.

Ponder: No one is useless in this world
who lightens the burden of it to anyone else.

Today I am grateful for

Shine bright

Ponder Time

Be the light

Have No Fear

Lots of people had such interesting stories
to tell after their losses when the tornadoes
struck Sunday, May 25. Most credited their
faith and prayers for saving their lives.
One woman had been to church in the morning and
the congregation sang, "Have No Fear, Little Flock."
The hymn's words kept running through her mind as
she was trapped under a cupboard, a chimney and walls.
A mother and three daughters were airlifted in their car and
the car was totaled but they had few injuries.
They thanked God for being found and alive.
The shock of the massive devastation was so overwhelming
but people responded to their needs immediately.
Even Parkersburg, West Virginia, their sister city, collected
$10,600 in less than 48 hours and sent it to the American
Red Cross Relief Fund. Most people felt but for the
grace of God it could have been them. After sorting through
the rubble of their homes one woman found her wedding ring
and some found a picture or other memento that filled them
with joy. Others were taking in lost pets or orphan animals
from the storm. Volunteer workers worked overtime to
provide for their basic needs.
The massive flooding in 83 counties of our state 2 weeks
later had the same reaction of volunteers and many service
organizations. They put in long hours to save as many
homes, businesses and people's lives as possible.
This is what Christianity is all about.
God says love your neighbor as yourself.
Through Christ our comfort overflows. 11 Corinthians 1:5

July 2008   187

Today I am grateful for

Ponder Time

Be the light

Time to Watch Out

When the Hebrew people had been led by
Moses through their darkest days, and now were
given hope for their future, he gave them strict
warnings. Deuteronomy 8: 11-13 Beware that in your plenty
you don't forget the Lord your God, and begin to disobey him.
For when you have become full and prosperous and have
built fine homes to live in and when your flocks and herds
have become very large, and your silver and gold have
multiplied, that is the time to watch out and don't become
proud, and forget the Lord your God.
Verse 19 But if you forget about the Lord your God and
worship other gods instead and follow evil ways, you shall
certainly perish, just as the Lord has caused other nations in
the past to perish. That will be your fate, too, if you don't obey
the Lord your God.
Is this what is happening to our country? We become proud
and think we did it all on our own and forget the Lord who has
blessed us with so many things. The morals and values
of our country are declining and Christians need to speak up
and bring our nation back to the laws our founding fathers
set up for us to adhere to.

"To get nations back on their feet, we must first
get down on our knees." Billy Graham

Ponder: Time flies, but remember ….. you are the navigator.

Today I am grateful for

All THINGS are POSSIBLE

Ponder Time

Be the light
✵✵✵✵✵✵✵✵✵✵✵

Colors of Nature

You can't see your reflection in a waterfall.
The water is in a constant state of motion.
But you can see your reflection in still waters.
The 23rd Psalm says, "He leads me beside still water,
he restores my soul." Another verse, Psalm 46:10, says,
"Be still and know that I am God."
Nature is changing color. Harvesting crops, plants and
flowers are arrayed in fall colors. Birds are starting to flock
together to migrate south and animals are
storing up for winter.
When we stop to see a pretty sunrise or sunset and take
notice of small details, like a small child would do, we are
drawn to God and appreciate all he has created.
Pause and give thanks for all he is doing for you.
James 4:8, "And when you draw close to God,
God will draw close to you."
We can be still and read his words, say prayers and listen
for his advice for us each day.

"Thou hast created all things, and for thy pleasure
they are and were created." Revelations 4:11

He has made everything beautiful in its time.
Ecclesiastes 3:11

Today I am grateful for

Choose Peace

Ponder Time

Be the light

Spirit of Willingness

When Abraham Lincoln was president
during the Civil War, a woman asked to see him.
He said, "What can I do for you?"
She replied, "I brought you some of your favorite cookies."
He was so touched. Everyone that came to see him
always had a request for something.
Does God feel the same way? Everyone thinks he is a
Heavenly Father and they all want a "give me this" and
"give me that."
God wants praise and thanks for all the blessings we take
for granted. There are so many destitute people affected by
hurricanes, tornadoes, war and under a tyrant's rule who are
in need of just the basic necessities.
We need to give back to God a contrite heart and a spirit of
willingness to serve him and worship him with praise and a
thankful heart.
Psalm 34:1-3 "I will praise the Lord no matter what happens.
I will constantly speak of his glories and grace. I will boast of
all his kindness to me. Let all who are discouraged take
heart. Let us praise the Lord together, and exalt his name."

You made my whole being .... I praise You because You
made me in an amazing and wonderful way.
Psalm 139: 13-14

Ponder: A good cook adds a pinch of love.

Today I am grateful for

Ponder Time

Be the light

We Can Be Assured

The angel Gabriel appeared to Mary
and his first words were, "Hail, O favored one.
The Lord is with you." Then he told her she would
give birth to Jesus (meaning Savior.)
Before his birth God appeared to Joseph, saying, "Behold
the virgin shall be with child and bear a Son, and they shall
call his name Emmanuel, which is translated,
"God with us." Matthew 1:23
These were troubling times in Israel. Rome ruled and
King Herod was an evil king,
and they were bogged down with taxes.
Here we are 2000 years later and look at the world now.
The Mideast is still in chaos. Our own country has been hit
hard with disaster this year and a plunging economy.
People have lost jobs, homes and securities.
No matter what our circumstances may be we can be
assured that God knew what he was doing when he sent
Jesus to save the world. His promises never fail that he will
always be with us. We often feel closer to God when we are
in the dark valleys but we can be assured if we put our trust
in him he promises us hope and peace.
My peace I give to you; not as the world gives do I give it
to you. Let not your hearts be troubled, neither let them
be afraid. John 14:27
Ponder: Contentment consists not in getting what you want,
but enjoying what you have.

Today I am grateful for

THE LORD IS MY
Light
AND
Salvation
PSALM 27:1

Ponder Time

Be the light

No Matter How Small

We just celebrated the birth of Christ.
God chose to have him come and dwell
among us as an infant, tiny and vulnerable--starting
small to accomplish the world's greatest good.
The Bible is full of instances where something small is made
into a miracle. Even a small seed planted will multiply. Jesus
took the boy's lunch of five loaves and two fish to feed 5,000.
His first miracle was changing water into wine.
When we start out as a Christian we are taking baby steps
but as we mature we grow in faith, love and in service.
The New Year depicts a baby in a diaper and ends with an
old man as Father Time.
We have a whole new year ahead of us to choose how we
will use God's word planted in us to share it with anyone who
doesn't know him. The world is in chaos and there is so much
need. Even what little we give adds up.
Even enough drops of water will fill a pail.
When we want to withdraw from difficult situations, nudge
us, Lord, to get us up and do something worthwhile,
no matter how small.

No eye has seen, no ear has heard, and no mind has
imagined what God has prepared for those who love Him.
Corinthians 2:9

Today I am grateful for

Ponder Time

Be the light

The Greatest Love

Could you have imagined when you were
born how long you would live and how you would die?
It's a good thing we can't or we would have a dark cloud
hovering over us all the time.
But Christ knew from the beginning why he was sent
and the suffering he would endure.
John 3:16 we can quote from memory, "For God so loved
the world that he gave his only begotten son that whosoever
believes in him should not perish but have everlasting life."
The first part is God so loved us that he was willing to have
his only Son be crucified for our sins. That is the greatest
love there is to do it on purpose.
Christ died for everyone, believers or not.
While Jesus was here on earth he was tempted, humiliated,
falsely accused, beaten, rejected and crucified, yet he
overcame all and followed through with the
mission he was sent for.
We can rejoice that he loved us so much that we can be
part of his family and his love never ends.

God has said, "I will never leave you;
never will I forsake you.." Hebrews 13:5

Today I am grateful for

Become the Change

Ponder Time

Be the light

Watch and Pray

Lots of people live alone, are shut-ins,
are away at college, are moving to a new place
or are going into the service away from home.
We all have felt lonely at some time and can even
feel alone in a crowd.
When Jesus began his ministry he spent forty days and
forty nights in the wilderness with no food or water.
Satan tempted him three times but Jesus quoted Scripture
and had him depart.
In this modern age of cell phones and text messages
we can't imagine anyone going forty days without
communication.
At Gethsemane the disciples were told to watch and pray.
Instead they went to sleep. At his trial they feared for their
own lives and deserted him.
But Jesus' biggest feeling of loneliness was dying on the
cross for our sins and God turning his back on him during
those six hours. One of his last sayings was, "My God, my
God, why have you forsaken me?"
This was the ultimate sacrifice to be abandoned during his
agonizing suffering. He paid the supreme sacrifice
for our redemption.
When you feel lonely, just think of what Jesus did for you
and be thankful.

I will not leave you comfortless: I will come to you.
John 14:18

Today I am grateful for

Let's make today beautiful

Ponder Time

Be the light

Our Own Anytime

God gave Moses the ten commandments
engraved on stone tablets. They were
placed in the Ark of the Covenant and its instruments
and were carried on poles while the Israelites were
wandering in the desert.
When they were later settled, King David had a nice cedar
palace and he thought the Ark of the Covenant should
have a cedar Temple instead of a tent. But God said, "No."
His son, Samuel, had the beautiful temple built. It took
7 years to build. The innermost sanctuary was closed
off by a curtain. Only a priest could go in and then come
out and speak to the people. Animals were sacrificed
for the people's sins.
When Jesus died on the cross and shed his blood, the
curtain in the Temple split apart from top to bottom. Now we
don't need an intercessor but can come to God on our own
anytime through prayer because of Jesus' sacrifice.
That proves how much he loves us and wants us to
draw near to him at any time.
"and when you draw close to God,
God will draw close to you." James 4:8

Ponder: The difference between a career and a job is
twenty or more hours a week.

Today I am grateful for

Believe in Yourself

Ponder This

Be the light

Guide Us

Jesus spent 3 years in close proximity
with his 12 disciples. When he knew his time
was drawing near for his death, he told them about it,
but of course they couldn't comprehend it.
Why would a young man, 33 years old,
who had performed so many miracles, talk about dying?
To ease their concerns he told them the Father would send
the Holy Spirit to dwell in them. He would be a comforter,
teacher, give them wisdom and power,
be a helper and an advocate.
After his death the Holy Spirit did come upon them and they
had power to preach and spread God's word to unbelievers
as they ministered for him.
We sing the Doxology every Sunday, "Praise Father, Son
and Holy Ghost," We can't see the Holy Spirit but we can feel
his presence. He is part of the Trinity and we can
be assured he dwells within us.
He was sent to guide us into all truth and to teach us.
We are empowered by the Spirit to witness, to pray and
to live a hope-filled life with love.
The Spirit also helps us in our weaknesses. For we do not
know what we should pray for as we ought. Romans 8:26
The Holy Spirit is worthy of our praise!

Ponder: Children need models more than they need critics.

Today I am grateful for

Ponder Time

Be the light

Time to Rethink

The talk now is all about conserving
and not wasting. This is not something new.
When Jesus fed the 5,000 he blessed the boy's
2 fish and 5 loaves of bread. After the people had plenty,
the disciples were told to pick up any leftovers and
they had 12 baskets full.
How was the fish cured to last all day? And there were no
preservatives in the bread.
The people dried fruit, made the grapes into wine and the
olives into olive oil.
Even the fishermen mended their nets. Their clothing had
to be handmade. There were no malls to go shopping.
Joseph and Mary had to flee to Egypt after Jesus was born.
What did she use for diapers while traveling with a
new infant?
The old timers were taught to conserve and save seed for
the next year's crop.
We have been a wasteful society and are caught up in a
downward economy. Much of the results we have brought
on ourselves. Even our health is at stake with high fats in
food and not much exercise.
It's time to rethink and conserve energy and
wasteful spending.

Ponder: Money never did buy happiness and credit cards
aren't doing much better.

Today I am grateful for

Shine bright

Ponder Time

Be the light

Compare Blessings

Afghanistan only gets 10" of rain in
a year so therefore they have no swimming pools
or water sports.
The terrain is mountainous and the war is still going on.
When we compare the blessings the Lord has provided
for us, we need to humbly thank him for a land that is free.
We are able to grow crops and produce to feed many.
We can see for miles in open country and our transportation
system excels theirs. No wonder their cash crop is opium.
They do have some crops and livestock but nothing
compared to ours. We don't have to flee to escape a war
going on and live in a refugee settlement.
It's summer now and more people are able to get
outdoors and enjoy activities these people can not.
Praise the Lord you can enjoy the summer.

Your life is God's gift to you;
What you do with it is your gift to God.

Give thanks unto the Lord; for He is good. Psalm, 136: 1
So many blessings to be humbly grateful for
in this beautiful season!

Today I am grateful for

Ponder Time

Be the light

Hold The Glory

We hear the word transparency more and
more in the news everyday. Our government is
now demanding open records that those in authority have
tried to conceal. We bail out the banks, auto industries,
insurance companies, etc., to solve their problems when
they were the ones at fault.
An Iowa Representative is accused of giving a false address
so his children could attend a certain school and avoid paying
higher tuition.
People cheat on their income taxes, pad expense accounts,
take bribes or ask for favors.
They think the rules don't apply to them.
Greed seems to be the underlying reason so many try it and
assume they will not get caught. But they will have to
answer to God someday.
We can't fool God. He knows every detail about us. We are
made in "his" image and he expects us to live up to his
standards and hold the glory of God inside us. When we let
God rule our lives then we are transparent to others and they
will see Christ living in us and be drawn to him.
"A good man is known by his truthfulness, and a false man
by deceit and lies." Proverbs 12:17

Ponder: Rare is the person who can weigh the faults of
others without putting his thumb on the scales.

Today I am grateful for

All THINGS are POSSIBLE

Ponder Time

Be the light

What Is Grace

We sing a familiar hymn, "Amazing Grace," but what is grace? Grace is God favoring us with blessings for which we did nothing. We can't earn his favors, he just bestows them.
We wake up every morning to a sunrise and every evening there's a sunset. He is ever present during the twenty four hour period and it is free to anyone regardless of race or creed.
When we call on him he listens, guides us with wisdom, touches us in many ways by calming our fears, provides mercy or comfort and gives us hope. He always loves us even if we sin and offers forgiveness. God is very patient with our everyday struggles and knows what is best for us. Sometimes he heals and sometimes it is not to be.
He tests our faith in many ways. If we withhold a kindness, nurse a grudge or dole out harshness, it displeases him very much. Often times we bring punishment upon ourselves because we don't obey and try to go our own way without his direction.
Grace is mentioned many times in the Bible. God is able to make all grace abound towards you. 2 Corinthians 9:8
Out of the fullness of his grace he has blessed us all, giving us one blessing after another. John 1:16
My grace is sufficient for you for my power is made perfect in weakness. 2 Corinthians 12:9

Praise God and give thanks for his grace.

Today I am grateful for

Choose Peace

Ponder Time

Be the light

Filling Up Our Cracks

Winter is around the corner and we
take special precaution to seal up cracks with
insulation, caulk, etc. to hold back the cold winds
and drafts. The Bible speaks in
1 Thessalonians 3:10 about filling up any little cracks
in our faith.
We all have to check our thoughts, attitudes, and motives
sometimes. Doubts and fears creep in and we worry and
become anxious about everyday circumstances. Our job,
health, regrets and the downward economy are ever before
us and it is hard to shrug off annoyances.
Psalms 37 is full of wisdom. Trust in the Lord. Be kind and
good to others, commit everything you do to the Lord. Trust
him to help you do it and he will. Rest in the Lord; wait
patiently for him to act. Stop your anger! Turn off your wrath.
Don't fret and worry as it only leads to harm.
The steps of good men are directed by the Lord. He delights
in each step they take. If they fall it isn't fatal, for the Lord
holds them in his hand. He will strengthen you.
Let us give thanks to God who gives us the strength and
hope to face each trial.

Ponder: Trouble is not a TRIAL, but a trust in God.

Some minds are like concrete,
thoroughly mixed up and permanently set.

Today I am grateful for

Ponder Time

Be the light

The Real Purpose

When Jesus was born in Bethlehem, some
shepherds were abiding in their fields guarding
their sheep. Suddenly an angel appeared among them,
and the glory of the Lord shone all around them. They were
frightened but the angel assured them, "Don't be afraid," he
said. "I bring you the most joyful news ever announced,
and it is for everyone! The Savior, yes the Messiah,
the Lord, has been born tonight in Bethlehem."
So why did the angel say Savior? It really goes back to the
Garden of Eden over 2000 years ago. Everything God made
was good and he could communicate with man.
That is until Adam and Eve sinned.
This has been man's downfall ever since.
Sacrificing animals for a blood offering did not make man's
heart contrite. Animals had to be sacrificed over and over
again but this did not appease God. So Jesus, his son, made
the supreme sacrifice with his blood and the old rituals were
not needed anymore. This was the greatest gift to mankind.
The wall separating man from God was broken.
We can now ask God for forgiveness for our wrongs.
The birth of Jesus is only a part of the wonderful story.
When we know the real purpose of his birth we can rejoice
in the greatest gifts from God.

Ponder: The task ahead of us is never as great as the
power behind us. Ralph Waldo Emerson

Today I am grateful for

THE LORD IS MY
Light
AND
Salvation

PSALM 27:1

Ponder Time

Be the light

Do Not Lose Heart

The school semester will soon be ending
and students are cramming for final exams
before their report cards are due.
Did you know God is keeping track of your life?
Psalms 139:6 "Every day of my life is recorded in your book."
Psalms 37:18 "Day by day the Lord observes the good deeds
done by Godly men and gives them eternal rewards."
Ecclesiastes 3:16 "In due season God will judge everything
man does, both good and evil."
1 Corinthians 5:10 "For we must all appear before the
judgment of Christ, so that each may receive good or evil,
according to what he has done in the body."
So what does your report card look like? How many times
are you absent from church, your conduct, effort, language
and good deeds?
We can all stand improvement and it is not too late to start
the New Year off with a desire to praise and please God.
He gives us so many blessings that we take for granted
but it can all change in a blink of an eye.
So let us not grow weary in well doing, for in due season
we shall reap if we do not lose heart.

PEOPLE ARE FUNNY...THEY WANT—
The Front seat in a bus,
The Center of the road, and
The Back seat in Church.

Today I am grateful for

Ponder Time

Be the light

Was Lost and Now Found

When you give someone a hug,
you stretch your arms out wide and draw the
person closer to you as you welcome them.
That's what Christ did on the cross. His arms were stretched
wide to welcome anyone to come to him,
and he also forgives them.
The story of the prodigal son is an earthly example.
The wayward son squandered all of his inheritance in
loose living. When he finally came to his senses he decided
to return home. His father saw him at a distance and
he ran and embraced him and kissed him and forgave him
for all of his sins.
The father is the important person in the story. He was so
happy to see his son because he thought he was dead and
now alive, was lost and now found. He didn't care what he
looked like or what he had done because
he rejoiced he was back.
Like the prodigal son, you have to make the effort on your
part to accept this free gift of salvation that Christ shed
his blood on the cross for you and he also forgives you.
His arms are always open to welcome you because
he loves you so much.

Ponder: God Himself does not propose to judge a man
until he is dead. So why should you?

Today I am grateful for

Become the Change

Ponder Time

Be the light

Prepare Your Way

John the Baptist was a relative of Jesus
and only a few months older. He knew from
his birth he was to prepare the way for the coming of
Jesus as the Messiah.
Imagine living in the wilderness, wearing clothes woven
from camel's hair, a leather belt and eating locusts and wild
honey. But he didn't resent any rivalry between them. As a
matter of fact he felt unworthy to baptize Jesus and was later
beheaded. He preached about the coming of Jesus and
many people were baptized in the Jordan River.
When Jesus knew his time was up to go to the cross, he set
his sights on going to Jerusalem. At the Garden of
Gethsemane he prayed for hours to prepare himself for what
he knew he had to do.
John the Baptist prepared the way for Jesus and Jesus
prepared himself for the crucifixion.
We go to great lengths preparing for celebrations and other
events in our lives.
Have you prepared for your way to Heaven by accepting
Christ as your Savior?
If not, don't waste any more time and then you can be
assured of this sacrificial gift.

Ponder: We don't change the message,
the message changes us.

Today I am grateful for

Let's make TODAY beautiful

Ponder Time

Be the light

Where I Am

When Jesus was born, Mary laid him
in a cold manger because there was no room
for them in the inn.
Bethlehem was crowded with people coming to register
for a census. Even today we are so busy with work,
pleasures, etc. we crowd out Jesus and have no room for him
in our lives.
Before Jesus left, he promised, "Let not your heart be
troubled; believe in God, believe also in me. In my Father's
house are many rooms, if it were not so, would I have told
you that I go to prepare a place for you? And when I go and
prepare a place, I will come again and will take you to myself,
that where I am you may be also."
What a difference there is between a lowly room in a stable
for Jesus' birth and the room he is preparing for believers in
Heaven. You can't begin to imagine what a room in Heaven
would look like and it would be permanent.
For those who reject him there will be a
permanent-No Vacancy.
So be sure you accept Jesus as your Savior
and don't delay.

SALVATION
Don't leave earth without it!

Today I am grateful for

Ponder This

Believe
in
Yourself

Be the light

Fulfilled Mission

When Jesus was born Mary pondered
all these things in her heart and often thought
how all of it had changed her life.
The family soon fled to Egypt for a couple of years
until King Herod was dead.
When Jesus was twelve he accompanied his parents to
Jerusalem for the Passover Festival. He didn't return with the
group and when his parents found him he was in the temple
discussing questions with the teachers of the law. His
response was. "Didn't you realize that I would be at the
temple, in my Father's house?"
Again Mary stored all these things in her heart.
Jesus was at home until he was thirty years old. He was the
wage earner in the family as a carpenter.
Mary was present when Jesus performed his first miracle
changing water into wine.
When he was crucified she had the heartbreak of watching
her son die a cruel death. Jesus asked his disciple John to
look after her and she went to live with him. She was
probably in her late forties or early fifties.
After Jesus rose from the dead Mary was put in the limelight
as she had fulfilled the mission she was sent for.

Ponder: Why are there so many old people in Church?
They're cramming for the final.

Today I am grateful for

Ponder Time

BE KIND

Be the light

Generational Changes

The word forty appears a number of times
in the Bible. It rained for forty days and forty nights
before the Ark floated. The Israelites roamed in the desert
for forty years before they could cross over to the Promised
Land. A man that was lame for forty years was healed.
Jesus appeared for forty days after his crucifixion.
We have reached a milestone of forty years when our two
churches and yoked churches merged June 1, 1970.
We are indebted to those early settlers back in 1865 and
1885 for their foresight and dedication for the need to worship
God our Creator.
The population of Winthrop was 150 people in 1865.
During these centuries there have been generations of
families to keep the love and sacrifice of Jesus alive and
strong. We have so many young families in our
congregation to prove it.
Times have changed over the years and with each
generation changes have been made to the structure of the
building. We are now in a new phase of an addition which will
be for the future generations. When the Lord builds a house
and blesses it, it will succeed. Happy 40th Anniversary!

Ponder: A lot of church members who are singing,
"Standing on the Promises" are just sitting on the premises.

Today I am grateful for

shine bright

Ponder Time

_____
_____
_____
_____
_____
_____
_____
_____
_____
_____
_____

Be the light

Sheeps Viewpoint

David is the writer of Psalm 23 but
He writes it from the viewpoint of a sheep.
A sheep will not be down in green pastures if it
is afraid, but when it sees the shepherd
it is assured everything is alright.
When the snow starts to melt in the mountains, the sheep
start their forage upward. The tableland is flat in the valley.
The shepherd goes ahead the day before and removes
poisonous weeds and clears the stream of winter debris
so the grass is at its best and the water is fresh.
There is always danger of coyotes, bears, cougars and
wolves looking down from the cliffs for a stray sheep or to
scare them and make them scatter.
The shepherd's staff and rod or club protects them.
Summer time is time for flies, mosquitoes, gnats and
winged parasites or scab. That is why the shepherd
anoints their heads with oil, especially around the nose.
Fall starts their descent and they know they are returning
to their home where they will dwell secure and know that
the shepherd is still watching over them.
No wonder this Psalm is a favorite,
as our Heavenly Father works out all the details
for our lives as well.

Ponder: Why didn't Noah swat those two mosquitoes?!

Today I am grateful for

TRUST THE TIMING OF YOUR LIFE

Ponder Time

Be the light

Got to Love Children

God has no grandchildren.
We are all a child of God.
The Apostle Paul's associate, Timothy, was
much younger than Paul and he addressed his letters
to him as my dear son. Timothy grew up to trust the Lord
just as his mother, Eunice, and his grandmother, Lois, did.
His early training he got at home was to love God
and to share his word with people.
Solomon was a wise king and wrote much of Proverbs. In
chapter 4 he says, "Young men, listen to me as you would
to your father. Listen, and grow up wise, for I speak the
truth–don't turn away. For I, too, was once a son, tenderly
loved by my mother and as an only child, the companion of
my father. He told me never to forget his words, "If you follow
them," he said, "you will have a long and happy life."
"Learn to be wise," he said, "and develop good judgment
and common sense."
Proverbs 22:6 states it best. "Train up a child in the way he
should go, and when he is old he will not depart from it."
We have so many young families and grandparents who
are following Christ's example and may God continue to
bless them in doing the right thing. We need more parents
and grandparents and friends to teach them.

Ponder: Children need love,
especially when they don't deserve it.

Today I am grateful for

All THINGS are POSSIBLE

Ponder Time

Be the light

My Friend

When we are born we are a child of God.
He is our Heavenly Father and Jesus is his son.
That makes Jesus our brother. Hebrews 22:11
Jesus has other names we can ascribe to him just like
we are to other people here on earth.
Another is friend, found in John 15:13. The greatest love is
shown when a person lays down his life for his friend, and
you are my friends if you obey me. I no longer call you
slaves, for a master doesn't confide in his slaves, now you
are my friend, proved by the fact that I have told you
everything the Father told me.
We are also joint heirs as in Romans 8:16-17. For his Holy
Spirit speaks to us deep in our hearts, and tells us that we
really are God's children. And since we are his children we
will share his treasures—for all God gives to his son Jesus is
now ours, too. But if we are to share his glory we must also
share his suffering.
More importantly, we should honor him as Lord, Master,
Good Shepherd, The Almighty God, Prince of Peace,
Creator and Everlasting Father.
These are royal titles due him. Be glad you are included in
the family of God.

Ponder: In the sentence of life, the devil may be a comma,
but never let him be the period.

Today I am grateful for

Choose Peace

Ponder Time

Be the light

Set An Example

Not many couples are mentioned in the Bible
but both Paul and Luke mention Aquila and Priscilla.
They were expelled from Italy not because they were
Christians but because they were Jews.
They sold their belongings and came to Corinth and
worked with Paul making tents. Priscilla probably learned
the Scriptures and writings growing up with her brothers
and could witness as well as her husband even though
women were held back in public. She was a gifted woman
and sometimes her name is mentioned first.
They traveled on ship with Paul, opened their home to
guests and held church in their home. All in all they were a
devoted ordinary couple who were always giving of
themselves to witness for Christ despite threats and
persecution. Once they risked their lives to save Paul.
They set an example for us by giving of their talents in
whatever way the Lord has blessed us.
Not what we say about our blessings,
but how we use them,
is the true measure of thanksgiving.

Ponder: Some people are kind, polite, and sweet-spirited
until you try to sit in their pews.

Today I am grateful for

you are
AMAZING

Ponder Time

Be the light

Service to Others

Recently the Crystal Cathedral, the mega church birthplace of the televangelist show, "Hour of Power," founded by Rev. Robert Schuller in the mid 50's in California, has filed for bankruptcy. They have a 30 million dollar mortgage and owe 7.5 million dollars to vendors.
A few years back Jim Baker, another televangelist, had a T.V. show P.T.L., before he was convicted of fraud and sent to prison.
This is a sharp contrast to compare these extremes to Jesus' birth. He was not born in a palace but an unheated stable with animals and his parents were not royalty but common people.
Jesus' whole life was one of service to others and he humbly washed the disciples' feet. He didn't have a home and walked for transportation and even the clothes on his back were taken from him at his crucifixion.
The Lord says, "Pride goeth before a fall," and we are seeing the results the world over.
The Lord wants a contrite heart.
Proverbs 18:12 Pride ends in destruction, humility ends in honor.

Ponder: It is easier to preach ten sermons than it is to live one.

Today I am grateful for

THE LORD IS MY
Light
AND
Salvation

PSALM 27:1

Ponder Time

Be the light

We Are On Fire

The story is told of a little church in a small town
that caught on fire. As most people do in a small town,
they stood around and watched it burn. The preacher went
around shaking hands with people.
He came to one man and said, "It's good to see you.
This is the first time I have seen you at church." the man
replied, "Preacher, this is the first time the
church has been on fire."
So, is our church on fire for the Lord? Indeed it is!
There is a big renovation of the building going on and
money has been given for this project. We are blessed with
Pastor Dean's excellent leadership and both a talented choir
and bell choir. All groups of the church are very active and
help with mission projects both locally and beyond.
The church is the people and
everyone does his or her part.
Wouldn't you agree we are on fire for the Lord?
Come and see for yourself.

Ponder: We are called to be witnesses,
not lawyers or judges.

Today I am grateful for

_____

_____

Ponder Time

Be the light

Love of the Will

AGAPE (ah GAH pay) – a Greek word for love used often in the New Testament (John 13:35; 1 Corinthians 13; 1 John 4: 7-18). Contrary to popular understanding, the significance of *agape* is not that it is an unconditional love, but that it is primarily a love of the will rather than the emotions. The New Testament never speaks of God loving unbelieving human beings with emotional love or a love that expects something in return. But He loves with His will (John 3:16; Romans 5:8). The reason for this is that God can find nothing enjoyable about a sinner on whom His wrath still abides. So He loves by His will, it is His nature to love. *Agape* love is Christ love. Marriages fail and friends drift apart but Christ's love lasts even into eternity. That's because He came down from Heaven as a babe and when He was an adult took upon himself all our sins, was crucified on a cross and redeemed us for our salvation. We must believe in Him and trust Him to come into our hearts to be assured of going to Heaven. Too many people have a love of earthy things and lose out on the day to day benefits of Christ's love. He gives peace, wisdom, hope for the future, patience, endurance, joy and much more. Once you accept Christ as Your Savior these things abound within you and continue to grow. Then you can share Christ's love with compassion and tell others about Him. Ponder: God doesn't call the qualified, He qualifies the called.

Today I am grateful for

Become the Change

Ponder Time

_____
_____
_____
_____
_____
_____
_____
_____
_____
_____
_____
_____

Be the light

The Need to Connect

When Jesus began his ministry he spent
40 days in the wilderness with prayer, fasting
and resisting the devil. He felt very deeply of being
prepared for the purpose for which he was sent.
After he called his disciples to follow him, he often withdrew
from them and spent time in prayer to God to keep up his
power as everyone wanted something from him.
They needed preaching, healing, to be fed, casting out
demons and he needed coping with the ridicule of the
Pharisees and authorities.
He often went to the hills to be alone and after he heard
John the Baptist was beheaded, he went out on a boat
alone. Another time he walked on the water
to meet their boat.
His last time of deep anguish and prayer to God was at
Gethsemane before he was arrested, the false trial and
crucifixion that lay ahead.
If Jesus felt the deep need of prayer as one who was
sinless, how much more should we who are guilty need to
connect to God in daily prayer.

Ponder: Don't put a question mark where God put a period.

Today I am grateful for

Let's make today beautiful

Ponder Time

Be the light

Faith Restored

In Mark 6:3 it lists Jesus' brothers:
James, Joseph, Judas and Simon, and sisters.
They are not mentioned at Christ's crucifixion,
only his mother, Mary, and other women watching from
a distance. The disciples were with him for three years and
they fled, except faithful John.
You would think one of the six immediate family members
would have cared for their mother.
But Jesus told John to care for her.
Isn't the family the first ones to take charge of a deceased
family member? We assume their father, Joseph, was
already dead and you would have thought they would
have had a family plot.
But no, the first one who got up courage to ask for his body
was Joseph from Arimathea, an honored member of the
Supreme Court, and also Nicodemus. He came and brought
a hundred pounds of embalming ointments made from myrrh
and aloes. Together they laid Jesus' body in a long linen cloth
saturated with the spices and placed him in an unused tomb
that was close by. Luke 19:38-42
Why did his family and friends desert him in a time of need?
We don't know but Jesus forgave everyone before he died.
Their faith was restored on Easter Sunday
when he arose from the dead.

Ponder: God promises a safe landing, not a calm passage.

Today I am grateful for

Believe in Yourself

Ponder This

Be the light

Second Chances

In the parable about the fig tree that
didn't yield any fruit, the owner wanted it cut down.
The gardener had an affection for it and he begged the
owner to give the tree a second chance. He wanted the
owner to reserve his judgment until he had tried everything
he could to have it yield. The gardener promises to
cultivate the soil and fertilize the ground giving the tree
every opportunity to produce figs.
The Bible is full of examples of God giving people a
second, third or more chances of redemption. The Hebrew
people complained about no food or water and worshiped
idols while in the desert. Peter denied Christ, Thomas
doubted and the woman committed of adultery was forgiven.
One of our greatest sins is pride.
We think we are self sufficient and forget about our creator.
We are also guilty of envy, jealousy, impure thoughts,
anger, losing our temper, lie or cheat, etc.
Praise the Lord he gives us another chance
after we repent
and learn from our mistakes.

Ponder: Opportunity may knock once,
but temptation bangs on your front door forever.

Today I am grateful for

Ponder Time

Be the light

What Will We Receive

Years ago the Smothers Brothers had a
TV show. After a chiding by Dick teasing Tommy,
he always replied, "Mom always liked you best."
The Bible tells of stories of favoritism by a parent
and the jealousy and hatred that followed.
One day in his old age, and half blind, Isaac told Esau, his
oldest son, to go and shoot a deer, cook it the way
he wanted and he would give the blessing that belonged to
him as the first born.
Rebekah overheard him and Jacob was her favorite so she
helped him deceive Isaac so Jacob would receive the
blessing. When Esau returned and found out he had been
tricked, he hated his brother.
Another story is of Jacob. He gave his favorite 17 year old
son, Joseph, a coat of many colors. Joseph had a dream that
someday his brothers would bow down to him. That made
them more jealous and hateful. When Joseph went to the
field to check on his brother, they wanted to kill him, but
instead sold him for slavery to some Ishmaelites in Egypt.
The Bible states that the Jews were God's favorite race
but when it comes to Judgement Day it is a different story.
"For we must all stand before Christ to be judged and have
our lives bared before him. For each will receive whatever
he deserves for the good or bad things he has done in his
earthly body. Act 10:34-35

Ponder: The best mathematical equation I have ever seen:
1 cross + 3 nails = 4 given.

Today I am grateful for

Shine bright

Ponder Time

_____

_____

_____

_____

_____

_____

_____

_____

_____

_____

_____

_____

Be the light

My Prayer Request

After King David died, his son, Solomon,
became king. The Lord appeared to Solomon
in a dream. He told him to ask for anything he
wanted, and it would be given to him.
Solomon answered, "Now that I have been made king
I feel like a child who doesn't know his way around. Give me
an understanding mind so that I can govern your people well
and know the difference between right and wrong.
For whom, by himself, is able to carry
such a heavy responsibility."
The Lord was pleased with Solomon's reply that he had
asked for wisdom. So he replied, "Because you have asked
for wisdom in governing my people, and have not asked for
a long life or riches for yourself, or the defeat of your
enemies, yes, I'll give you what you asked for. I will give you
a wiser mind than anyone has ever had or will have! And I will
also give you what you didn't ask for, riches and honor! And
no one in the world will be as rich and famous as you are for
the rest of your life."
Then Solomon woke up and realized it was a dream
but it became a reality in his life.
Did you notice that his prayer request was for others and
not himself? Most of today's people want "Give me and not
what can I do for others. We need to heed this message.

Ponder: If it's true that we are here to help others,
then what exactly are the others here for?

Today I am grateful for

TRUST
THE
TIMING
OF
YOUR
LIFE

Ponder Time

Be the light

Our Welcome Mat

We have been on vacation all year but
like any vacation it is always nice to be home.
The Lord was with us during these months
and we were very appreciative of our host church,
St. Patrick's Catholic Church, Winthrop, Iowa.
An outstanding feature in their church is all the many
stained glass windows, each depicting a Biblical story.
They are truly a work of art to incorporate all these
intricate pieces and then inlay them.
Many churches have stained glass windows, including ours.
When the light shines through the windows
they are really beautiful.
Each stained glass could represent a person serving the
Lord. 1st Peter 4:10 says, "God has given each of you some
special abilities, be sure to use them to help each other,
passing on to others God's many kinds of blessings. Do it
with all the energy and strength God supplies so that
God will be glorified through Jesus Christ."
We have seen all the many acts of talent and kindness
during this remodeling project and we praise the Lord.
"Let your light shine before men so that they may see your
good works and glorify your Father who is in heaven."
Matthew 5:16
The welcome mat is out. Come and join us.

Ponder: I don't know why some people change churches:
what difference does it make which one
you stay home from?!

Today I am grateful for

All things are possible

Ponder Time

_____

_____

_____

_____

_____

_____

_____

_____

_____

_____

_____

Be the light

Coming Together

Our church united the two denominations,
United Church of Christ and United Methodist
Church, and formed the Church of Christ United
forty one years ago, in June of 1970.
This is a good record and it's still going strong.
If you remember Moses went up on Mt. Siani and stayed
forty days and nights and the Lord gave him the
Ten Commandments written on stone tablets. While he was
gone the people thought he wasn't coming back and they
made a golden calf to worship and were dancing.
When Moses came down from the mountain he saw them
and was so angry with the people he threw the tablets to
the ground and they broke. Later he returned with two more
stone tablets and God wrote the commandments again.
Since this first generation and Moses disobeying God,
they were in the desert for forty years and did not get to
cross over into the Promised Land. The second generation,
under Joshua, crossed over and God blessed them.
In the forty one years we have been together there are
several families of third generation attending and more new
families are coming. The Lord has truly blessed us with a
newly remodeled church and a united congregation
coming together in worship and service.
Praise the Lord!

Ponder: It's not hard to meet expenses, they're everywhere.

Today I am grateful for

Choose Peace

Ponder Time

Be the light

What Will You Get Back

Years ago a lady and her family lived
in a neighborhood where her next door
neighbors were gossipy, malicious and had no
respect for anyone's property.
The lady had a peach tree that was shading
the kitchen window of these people.
The peach tree produced only hard green peaches that
never matured. They were good for only one thing—throwing
and you can guess whose boys threw them and where.
The lady decided to cut down the peach tree and plant
some flowers there.
When the neighbor heard it they rushed over to have her
spare the tree since it was the only shade for their kitchen.
She said, "Of course, I will leave the tree."
When spring came the next year a strange thing happened.
The tree was full of blossoms that resulted in a huge harvest
of sweet delicious fruit.
She gave away to all the neighbors and canned a lot.
The lady could have had revenge but she forgave the
family, and saw the results.
"Judge not, and you will not be judged. Give, and it will be
given to you: good measure, pressed down, shaken together,
running over, will be put into your lap. For the measure you
give will be the measure you get back." Luke 6:38
Ponder: You can tell how big a person is by what it takes to
discourage them.

Today I am grateful for

Ponder Time

Be the light

Bringing Joy

The New Testament uses the word "joy"
and "joyful" sixty one times. Usually the word
ascribes the way the believer feels when
he lives his life in Christ.
Jesus says, "Things I have spoken to you that my joy
may be in you and that your joy may be full."
That first Christmas when Jesus was born, Mary was
overjoyed that the long trip riding sidesaddle on a donkey
was over. Every step the donkey made she was aware of
and there was no back support. Every night was restless in
a strange surrounding and wondering when and where
Jesus would be born.
They definitely had their privacy even in a stable.
No wonder she was filled with joy at his birth.
The angels in heaven praised God and sang,
"Peace on earth for all those pleasing him."
The shepherds were afraid but the angel said, "I bring you
the most joyful news ever announced and it is for everyone.
The Savior, yes, the Messiah, the Lord, has been born
tonight in Bethlehem."
Share this joyful news and bring joy to those who need it.

Ponder: When you get to your wit's end,
you'll find God lives there.

Today I am grateful for

THE LORD IS MY
Light
AND
Salvation
PSALM 27:1

Ponder Time

262

Be the light

Doing It

Practice makes perfect, but be careful what you practice. It will become a habit.

All the great athletes, musicians, and for any accomplishment in life, one has spent hours in dedication to achieve their goal.

Habits start out doing IT a little BIT until IT becomes a HABIT. Many habits are hard to break and can injure your health, cause accidents and lose your good name and be a disgrace to your family.

Some people swear or lose their temper and are abusive without thinking. Driving while using cell phones, texting, drinking and speeding are bad habits and are causing traffic accidents and deaths.

Try practicing good habits. Even a smile, courtesy or a good deed can lift someone else's spirit.

Lao Tzu says, "Watch your thoughts; they become words.
Watch your words; they become actions.
Watch your actions; they become habits.
Watch your habits; they become character.
Watch your character; it becomes your destiny.

Ponder: He who angers you, controls you!

Today I am grateful for

Ponder Time

Be the light

What's Our Motives

Love is universal. Even if there is a
language barrier, a kindness can bring a smile.
The children we sent Operation Christmas Shoe Boxes
to we will never meet but their joy speaks volumes.
The local food boxes were much appreciated at
Thanksgiving and at Christmas.
Those donating blood will never meet the recipient
but it saved a life.
Even animals know when they are loved and cared for.
The shelter is full of abused pets, and their pitiful eyes
tell their sad story.
This year with the downward economy, more people
stepped up to help. They paid someone's layaway bill,
dropped money in the Salvation Army kettle and
helped in big and small ways.
Christmas is over but the need continues.
1st Corinthians 15:14 Do all your work in love.
Deuteronomy 6:5 Love the Lord your God with all your
heart, with all your soul, and with all your strength.
Proverbs 21:2 We can justify our every deed,
but God looks at our motives.
Love is not words alone, so put it into action.
We might be the one needing it.

Ponder: Don't give God instructions-just report for duty!

Today I am grateful for

Become the Change

Ponder Time

Be the light

Hour Of Need

Everyone feels rejection at some time
in their life. Maybe it was a friend who let you down,
a date refused, a job offer rejected, someone else
got credit or was promoted instead of you, a divorce, etc.
All these are hurtful but nothing compares to all the rejection
Christ endured. Even his home town refused to accept him
as the Messiah, including his family.
The Scribes and Pharisees were always trying to trip him
up with a trick question and ready to incite a mob.
At the end of his life his disciples were no true friends as
Judas betrayed him and Peter denied him and most left him
in his hour of need. When Jesus was brought to trial
they hid and almost all did not follow him to the cross.
They were afraid for their own lives.
They didn't attend his funeral, either.
So what kind of friends were they?
So if we think our lives are in turmoil, think of what Jesus
endured with beatings, mocking and enduring the agony
and suffering on the cross for us.

Ponder: Today on Twitter, I lost a follower.
Now I know how Jesus feels everyday.

Today I am grateful for

Let's make today beautiful

Ponder Time

Be the light

Step Out In Faith

At the Last supper no servants were
available so Jesus the host, humbled
himself and washed the disciples' feet.
After he served the last meal with them both Judas and
Peter are the conspicuous sinners. Judas betrayed him
but it was a deliberate sin and he left in the outer darkness.
Peter denied him three times but each was on the
spur of the moment. When he realized what he had done
he wept bitterly.
Jesus knew how much love each had after spending three
years with them. They had enjoyed his blessings and had
seen the miracles he performed. For Peter, he forgave him,
and he began a ministry of devotion to tell people about
the risen Christ.
No one is perfect and we all make choices. We make
promises of what we will do but it doesn't always materialize.
We don't want to admit our weakness or need and
pride gets in the way.
God looks on the heart and is willing to forgive us
and will give us strength and the hope to
step out in faith and serve him.
Remember decisions made in a moment
can affect a lifetime.

Ponder: Did Noah include termites on the ark?

Today I am grateful for

Believe
in
Yourself

Ponder This

Be the light

Go and Make Disciples

After Jesus rose from the dead the eleven disciples left for Galilee, going to the mountain where Jesus had said they would find him. There they met him and worshiped him–but some weren't sure it was really Jesus! He told his disciples, "I have been given all authority in heaven and earth. Therefore go and make disciples in all the nations, baptizing them into the name of the Father and of the Son and of the Holy Spirit and then teach these new disciples to obey all the commands I have given you; and be sure of this–that I am with you always, even to the end of the world."

Now that they were given this new command, did they have families? We know Peter was married because Jesus healed his mother-in-law. Paul wrote to the people in Corinth, "If I had a wife, and if she were a believer, couldn't I bring her along on these trips just as the other disciples do, and as the Lord's brothers do and as Peter does?"

The women can now get involved in spreading God's word. Before this they weren't mentioned much. Thanks to all these early believers for their sacrifices so we could become followers.

Ponder: If a church wants a better pastor, it only needs to pray for the one it has.

Today I am grateful for

BE KIND

Ponder Time

Be the light

How to Honor Him

Fathers' Day is June 17 and we
give tribute to our earthly fathers.
But we also have a Heavenly Father.
He has made us and provides us with so much
on a daily basis.
So what can we do to honor Him?
He really "spoils" us. He gives us so much we take for
granted–the air we breathe, rest, good health, grace,
comfort, forgiveness, nature to enjoy, food supply,
free country and freedom to worship.
The list is endless and yet we complain.
He prefers our praise and thanks.
Just spend some time each day, reading His word and
serving Him in any way possible.
Take some extra time and enjoy His company.

Ponder: The good Lord didn't create anything without a
purpose, but mosquitoes come close.

Today I am grateful for

Shine bright

Ponder Time

Be the light

Wake Up Call

King David wanted to build a temple
for God but God said, "no," but his son Solomon
was allowed to do it.
The temple was 90' long, 30' wide and 45' high.
The stones used in the construction of the temple were
prefinished at the quarry, so the entire structure was built without
the sound of hammer, axe or any other tool at the building site.
Figures of angels, palm trees and open flowers were carved on all
the walls. The walls and ceiling in the inner room were pure gold
and the floor was overlaid with gold. This room was where
the Ark of the Covenant was placed.
The curtains were made from linen and woven in different colors.
It took 7 years to build and 13 more years to build
Solomon's palace.
The Lord blessed it and told the people to remain true to Him.
But as it happened, Solomon married other girls who worshiped
goddesses of their tribes and he did, too. God was very angry and
later had their city and Temple destroyed.
Does this sound like the world now? It is in chaos and some
people have no respect for God or one another. There are more
wars, earthquakes and disasters than ever before.
This is a wakeup call to turn back to God.

"May the Lord **bless** you and keep you,
May the Lord make his face **shine** upon thee and be
gracious unto thee:
May the Lord turn his face toward you and give you **peace**."
Numbers 6:24- 26

Ponder: If God is your co-pilot - swap seats.

Today I am grateful for

TRUST THE TIMING OF YOUR LIFE

Ponder Time

Be the light

On your journey of life, may you have
many grace-filled opportunities to
shine brightly.

This light bringing
servers journal
belongs to:

Faith

Peace

_____

_____

_____

_____

_____

I have grown in grace and faith and have
completed another growth ring that is
connected to my legacy.

2 Corinthians 13:14

Ponder Time
_/_/_

Renew your soul

He-*arts* to Hearts
Where **YOU**
become the
Legacy Keeper
Time to pass it on!